A T L A N T A

MUSIC
INDUSTRY
CONNECTION

resources for:

ARTISTS
PRODUCERS
MANAGERS

by
JAWAR

1

"Know Thyself" Kemetic Proverb

Copyright 2004-2006 Music Industry Connection, LLC
ISBN: 0-9759380-1-0
Library of Congress Control Number

by JaWar

SECOND EDITION-REVISED AND UPDATED

Published by

Music Industry Connection, LLC
P.O. Box 52682, Atlanta, GA 30355, USA
800-963-0949 www.mt101.com questions@mt101.com

Printed in the U.S.A.

Cover Design: Derrick Leslie of Next Level Entertainment
Edited by Seneferu Ast
Interview transcribed by Candice Monique Butler

3

ACKNOWLEDGEMENTS

Writing and publishing the second edition of the Atlanta Music Industry Connection Book has been a learning experience. Because of the first edition I have met a number of fantastic people, created new windows of opportunity and created new pipelines of marketing and distributing my intellectual property. A special thanks to everyone that purchased a copy of the first edition, to the retailers that supported my efforts and to friends and family that want let me go homeless again. I do appreciate you!

The Most High, the Ancestors, Baba Moorise, Mona Fenderson, Linwood Fenderson, Maurice Beatty, Big Josh, Jeremy Jaws, Janae, Maurice Beatty, Granny, Kiesha, Uncle Tony, Aunt Helen, Aunt Hattie, Auntie Marion, Auntie Marva, Kimma, Cousin Tony, Uncle Paul, Adrienna Beatty, Willie Hunter, Ray Hamilton, TJ Chapman, Barry Brown, Bro. Silas, Cawasdis Brooks, Cool Water, Dee Mello, Desmick Perkins, DJ New York City Ken, Drummer Boi, Gordon Mills, Hotep, Jamilah Davis, Joe-Lynwood, K. Pat, Landrum, Leticia, Mike Lowery, Moses Hardin, Nicole, Omara Harris, John Christmas, Veda Cherry, Parrish Johnson, Philip Rodgers, Sean Stanley, Stephen Strother, Tyler Briant, Veronica Wilson, Bem, Xavier Baker, Dayo Adebiyi, Richard Dunn, Brad McDonald, Dee Dee Cocheta, DJ Brad, Reggie Regg, Janice, Jocelyn Vickers, Vonda Thomas, Joe aka Adobe, James Hickman, Cirocco, Coriya Burns, Dante Marshall, DeAngelo Muhammad, Dedra Davis, DJ Dagwood, DJ Knotts, DJ Dre, Empress Raw, Eric Page, Haziq, Glen Gordon, Greg Street, Hasson Diggs, Ian Burke, Islam, Keenan Gordon, Desiree, Power Born, Renee Atkins, Allen Johnston, Robert White, Ronesia, Rovella, Scott Keniley, Seven, Shameka, Melvin, Mi Mi, Tammy Allen, Tariq, Tony Baraka, AKA-Tay, G-Code, Chaka Zulu, Kim, Fort Knox, Karl Washington and Joseph Arrington. I didn't forget you I just didn't have enough room; please include your name here!

My goal is to provide a how to resource tool, reference guide and directory for artists, producers, managers and other music business professionals involved in the Growing Atlanta Music Industry and to increase awareness for businesses engaged in the Atlanta Music Industry Dynamic. In addition, the book is designed to give aspiring artists, producers and managers practical steps and tips for achieving their goals and realizing their success.

DEDICATIONS

This book is dedicated to Cousin Donnie Brown-one of the best singer/songwriter/music producers the world may never know rest easy cousin I miss you, being homeless, sleeping on floors, not having any money, being home sick, unpaid student loans, bounced checks, maxed out credit cards, the lawyer who offered me 10% to publish the first edition of this book when it was already selling in book and music stores, to the member of the legendary hip hop group who stole my copyrights and plagiarized my intellectual property to the first edition of this book, breached contract and acted in unethical business practices, to the women who thought I should give them a complimentary copy of my book because they were cute: if the P ain't free; then the book cost money oh yeaaah, to those who want something for nothing, to sleepless nights, to hunger pains, to credit reporting agencies that report inaccuracies and incompleteness and to those who said I couldn't, I did and there is more to come.

These are but a few of the motivating factors that were on my heart, mind and spirit while updating the second edition of the Atlanta Music Industry Connection Book: Resources for Artists, Producers and Managers.

TABLE OF CONTENTS

ARTIST DEVELOPMENT

- What Is A Performing Rights Organization? 9
- How Do I Contact A Pro? 10
- Recording Studios 10
- Where May I Get A U.P.C. Barcode? 21
- How May I Get A Parental Advisory Label? 21
- How Do I Contact The RIAA? 22
- CD, DVD & Vinyl Manufacturers 22
- Printers For Flyers & CD-Inserts 24
- Digital Distribution Companies 28
- Distribution Companies............................31
- Getting Your Own Website......................33
- Photographers...................................33
- Music Conferences 35
- How Do I Find More Shows To Perform In? 37
- Talent Show/Open-Mic Organizers 38
- Creating Your Own Talent-Show..........................40
- Record Companies 42
- How To Market Your Independent Release..........48
- When do I need a manager? 50
- How should I select a qualified manager? 50
- When do I need an entertainment attorney?..........51
- How should I select an entertainment attorney? 51
- How much do attorney fees cost? 52
- Artist's Revenue Streams.............................52

PRODUCER'S WORKSHOP

- What Equipment Do I Need? 53
- How Do I Insure My Equipment? 53
- When Do I Need An Entertainment Attorney?   54
- Recording Studios 55
- Music Equipment & Gear Stores 56
- Augusta Music Equipment Stores 60
- Music Conferences...............................60

➢ Mastering Facilities 61
➢ Producer Websites Of Interest 63
➢ How Should A Producer Market Their Tracks? 63
➢ Producer's Revenue Stream 64

MANAGER'S CORNER

➢ What skills do I need to succeed as a manager? 69
➢ What are the three types of managers?...................69
➢ Who pays the manager? 70
➢ How much money are artist managers paid?..........70
➢ When do I need an entertainment attorney?...........71
➢ May the manager also be the artist's attorney?......71
➢ How do I find new talent? 71
➢ Management Companies 72
➢ Management Books 76
➢ Management Organizations.....................................77
➢ Interview with Dayo & Al of Own Music..............78
➢ Manager's Revenue Stream 88

INFORMATION FOR ALL

➢ Six ways to protect yourself in the industry...........89
➢ What Copyright Forms do I need? 89
➢ Obtain copyright forms through 89
➢ What is the price to register a copyright?...............90
➢ How do I protect my band name & logo in GA?....90
➢ How do I contact the GA Secretary of State? 90
➢ How do I protect my band name and logo in the
   United States?...90
➢ When do I need a business license or Tax I.D.? 91
➢ What is the difference between a business
   license and a Tax I.D.? 91
➢ How do I get a business license?............................91
➢ What is a tax I.D.?..91
➢ How do I get a tax I.D.? 91
➢ What is Dun & Bradstreet? 92
➢ How may I contact Dun & Bradstreet? 92
➢ Where may I get business cards for free? 92
➢ How may I get flyers printed for free? 92

➤ How may I get 50 to 100 Promo CDs FREE? 93
➤ Where may I use the Internet for free? 94
➤ How may I get a free e-mail account? 94
➤ What is a One-Sheet? 94
➤ What is a Split Sheet? 95
➤ What is Soundexchange? 95
➤ How do I contact Soundexchange? 95
➤ Where Do Music Professionals Network? 96
➤ Music Retail Stores 96
➤ What Is Consignment? 97
➤ Who Tracks And Monitors Radio Airplay? 105
➤ Contacting BDS, Media Guide & Mediabase 105
➤ College & Community Radio 105
➤ Commercial Radio 109
➤ Internet Radio Stations 111
➤ Music & Entertainment Magazines 112
➤ How To Use Record Pools To Test-Market
   Your Next Hit 114
➤ Record Pools & DJ Organizations 116
➤ What Is Soundscan? 117
➤ Marketers & Promoters 120
➤ Internet Resource Guide 122
➤ Graphic Design Companies 122
➤ Music Consultants 124
➤ Music Organizations 126
➤ Entertainment Attorneys 128
➤ Video Production Companies 133
➤ Music Video Shows 141
➤ Music Business Books 143
➤ Atlanta Clubs & Venues 144
➤ Creating Wealth 147
➤ Learn How To Publish Your Own Book 165
➤ About The Author 168

ARTIST DEVELOPMENT

What is a Performing Rights Organization?

A Performance Rights Organization or PRO is an organization responsible for collecting & distributing performance royalties (money) to songwriters and music publishers. For example, whenever you hear a public broadcast of a song (i.e. radio, T.V. commercial jingle, music heard while on hold or at a concert venue, elevator music, music played in department stores and malls) you are hearing a public broadcast of music. The companies that broadcast the music are required to obtain a license for using this music. They obtain a license from (pay money to) one, two or all of the three PRO's. The PRO's, in turn, pay all or some of the money to its member songwriters and music publishers.

In addition to collecting money on behalf of songwriters and publishers, a performance rights organization is great for learning and networking in the music business.

The performance rights organizations have regular talent showcases, music business panel discussions, and songwriting clinics that help nurture songwriters and strengthen their knowledge base on the music industry. The networking opportunities available through a performance rights organization cannot be overstated.

How do I contact a PRO?

- ASCAP-American Society of Composers,
  Authors and Publishers
  PMB-400, 541 10th Street NW, Atlanta, GA 30318
  P) 404-351-1224
  www.ascap.com

- BMI-Broadcast Music, Inc.
  3340 Peachtree Rd., NE, Suite 570, Atlanta, GA 30326
  P) 404-261-5151 F) 404-816-5670
  www.bmi.com
  atlanta@bmi.com

- SESAC
  55 Music Square East, Nashville, TN 37203
  P) 615-320-0055
  www.sesac.com

RECORDING STUDIOS

An artist or producer should determine the goal, create a practical plan and rehearse the plan before paying studio costs to record. This will save a great deal of time and money.

There is a wide range of studios at your disposal. When it comes to recording, a good rule of thumb is the fewer the surprises, the better off you are. With that in mind, one of the questions you will want to ask is if the quoted price includes the studio engineer's fee, as sometimes it does and sometimes it doesn't, so remember to ask. In addition, many studios offer block (discount) rates when you book (reserve) say 10 or more hours at a time. Therefore, it is to your advantage to block out studio time to save money. However, if you are not accustomed to recording for 10 hours then this may be a waste of time and money. Studio prices may range from $35/hr to $200/hr.

Remember to bring your own CD-Rs and other record-able devices to the studio. The studio will probably have some on hand, but it will cost you a lot more money to buy it from the studio rather than to bring your own. Remember, the recording studio is in business to make a profit, so they are going to make every penny they can. In addition, to studio cost you want to ask about the experience of the studio engineer that will work on your project and the style of music the studio normally records. Ideally, you'll also want to ensure that there is chemistry between you and the engineer. In summary, a few factors to consider before choosing a studio are: **studio cost, experience of studio engineer, whether the engineer records your style of music often and chemistry between artist, producer & studio engineer.** When contacting the recording studios below let them know that you found them in the Atlanta Music Industry Connection Book by JaWar.

- 2201 Studios
  2459 Roosevelt Hwy, Ste. C-5, College Park, GA 30337
  P) 404-762-5744
  www.2201studios.com
  info@2201studios.com

- 2 High Recording Studios
  540 Permalume Place, Atlanta, GA 30318
  P) 404-603-9771 F) 404-475-0618
  www.2highstudios.com
  info@2highstudios.com

- 2ND 2 Nunn Recording Studio
  1558 North Highway 27, Carrollton, GA 30117
  P) 770-214-1707 P) 866-208-3505
  www.2nd2nunn.com
  studio@2nd2nunn.com

- 302 Entertainment
  850 Marcus Hyah Ct., Atlanta, GA 30349
  P) 770-909-7202

- 4th Generation Productions
  3140 Mangum Ln., SW, Atlanta, GA 30311
  P) 404-691-6493
  www.105entertainment.com

11

jimmyswagger@hotmail.com

- 500 Grand Studios
  Contact: Carlos Foreman
  1850 Graves Rd., Suite 215, Norcross, GA 30093
  P) 770-985-8354

- ACA Digital Recording, Inc.
  P.O. Box 450727, Atlanta, GA 31145
  P) 404-284-0948 F) 404-284-7429

- Air Tyte Recordings
  312 Collier Rd., Barnesville, GA 31145
  P) 770-358-7552

- All Good Productions
  120 Interstate Pkwy., Suite 164, Atlanta, GA 30339
  P) 770-956-9698 P) 877-294-0863
  www.allgood.net

- APC Recording Studios
  3838 Oakcliff Industrial Court, Atlanta, GA 30340
  P) 770-242-7678
  www.apcstudios.com
  stuff@apcstudios.com

- Arcadia Recording Studio
  4540-B South Berkeley Lake Road, Norcross, GA 30071
  P) 770-448-9992
  www.arcadiarocks.com
  info@arcadiarocks.com

- Big Cat Studios
  500 Bishop St., Suite E5, Atlanta, GA 30318
  P) 404-603-8229 P) 404-438-7371

- Bizzi Beats Studios
  3274 E. Main St., College Park, GA 30337
  P) 404-259-4352
  www.bizzibeats.com
  sta_bizzibnt@hotmail.com

- Blackberry Recordings

3141 E. Ponce DeLeon Ave., Scottdale, GA 30079
P) 678-361-0692
blackberrysounds@aol.com

- Blue Sound Studios
P.O. Box 191141, Atlanta, GA 31119-1141
P) 404-327-4228 P) 877-327-4228 F) 404-327-7769
www.bluesoundstudios.com
info@bluesoundstudios.com

- Blue Studio Productions
4925 Lakeside Dr., Atlanta, GA 30360
P) 770-451-3007
www.thebluestudio.com
office@thebluestudio.com

- Caber Media
126 N. Peachtree St., Norcross, GA 30071
P) 404-520-5055
www.cabermedia.com
info@cabermedia.com

- Captive Sound Recording Studio
1442 Tullie Rd NE, Atlanta, GA 30329
P) 404-325-4860
www.captivesound.com

- Catspaw Productions
922 Curie Drive, Alpharetta, GA 30005
P) 678-624-7660 P) 888-807-2639 F) 678-624-7557
www.catspawproductions.com
info@catspawproductions.com

- Cherry Recording Studios
800 East Ave NE, Atlanta, GA 30312
P) 404-524-7757

- Claymore Studios
2459 Roosevelt Highway, Suite B-16
College Park, GA 30337
P) 404-762-5021 F) 404-762-5524
www.landmine-ent.com

- CMO Studio
  2310-D Marietta Blvd., Atlanta, GA 30318
  P) 404-355-0909 F) 404-352-2136
  www.cmopro.com
  cmopro@cmopro.com

- Compound Recording Studio
  222 Peters St., Atlanta, GA 30313
  P) 404-526-9832
  otsrecords@bellsouth.net

- Creative Sound Concepts
  1495 Northside Dr., Suite D, Atlanta, GA 30318
  P) 404-873-6628 F) 404-367-9599
  creativesound@mindspring.com

- DMC Productions
  P.O. Box 2253, Stockbridge, GA 30281
  P) 404-931-4373 P) 404-964-7026 F) 734-448-2968
  www.dmcpro.net

- Doppler Recording Studios
  1922 Piedmont Circle, Atlanta, GA 30324
  P) 404-873-6941 F) 404-249-7148
  www.dopplerstudios.com
  info@dopplerstudios.com

- Down 4 Life Recording Studios
  5127 Old National Hwy, Atlanta, GA 30349
  P) 404-766-7377

- Earcandy Recording
  204 W. Poplar St., Suite A, Griffin, GA 30224
  P) 770-228-2066
  www.earcandyrecording.com

- Exocet Recording Studios
  3264 Shallowford Rd, Chamblee, GA 30341
  P) 770-455-7256 F) 770-457-5243
  www.exocetstudios.com
  info@exocetstudios.com

- Gibson Recording

595 Huntwick Pl., Roswell, GA 30075
P) 770-518-0404 F) 404-843-4334

- Golden Boy Recording Studios
  5319 Old National Hwy, College Park, GA 30349
  P) 404-684-5999 F) 404-684-5973

- Gold Cast Recording
  485 West Crossville Rd., Roswell, GA 30075
  P) 678-886-3353
  Jimmyet2005@yahoo.com

- Go-Town Studios
  2093 Faulkner Rd., NE, Atlanta, GA 30324
  P) 404-325-0882 F) 404-325-0196
  www.cash-awn.com
  ccahsoon@yahoo.com

- Group Effort Studios
  842 Marietta St., Atlanta, GA 30318
  P) 770-633-0050
  www.groupeffortstudios.com
  booking@groupeffortstudios.com

- House 21 Entertainment Recording Studio
  2100 Drake Court, Lithonia, GA 30058
  P) 678-508-3742

- JFX Studio
  1823 Tree Top Way, Marietta, GA 30062
  P) 770-977-0982
  www.jfxstudio.com

- Joi Recording Studios
  2356 Park Central Blvd., Decatur, GA 30035
  P) 678-418-9973 F) 678-418-9954
  581@bellsouth.net

- Hot Beats Recording Studios
  1200 Spring St., Atlanta, GA 30309
  P) 404-379-7126
  www.hotbeatsatl.com
  hotbeatl@mac.com

- LedBelly Sound Studio
  P.O. Box 2202, Woodstock, Georgia 30188
  P) 770-345-0908 F) 770-345-9639
  www.ledbellysound.com
  Matt@LedBellySound.com

- Lighthouse
  2966 Winn Drive, Lawrenceville, GA 30044
  P) 770-381-7106
  http://members.aol.com/lhsestudio

- Mayday Sound Studio
  3875 Green Industrial Way, #600, Chamblee, GA 30341
  P) 770-457-5551
  maydaysound@earthlink.net

- Maze Recording Studio
  741 Lambert Dr., Atlanta, GA 30324
  Cell) 770-633-5747
  derrick@mazestudios.net

- McMix
  2878 Jonquil Dr., Smyrna, GA 30080
  P) 770-436-9620
  www.mcmix.com
  mcmix@mcmix.com

- Morrow House Studios
  251 Bighton Way, Marietta, GA 30066
  P) 770-422-3859
  www.morrowhousestudios.com
  max@morrowhousestudios.com

- National Recording Corporation
  P.O.Box 5111, Rome, GA 30162
  P) 706-234-4864
  www.narecorp.com
  info@narecorp.com

- Nickel & Dime Recording Studios
  106 N. Avondale Rd., Avondale Estates, GA 30002
  P) 404-297-0955
  www.nickelanddimestudios.net

- Night Sky Music
  223 Manley Rd., Griffin, GA 30223
  P) 770-229-5554
  www.nightskymusicstudio.com

- Oasis Recording Studio
  750 Ralph McGill Blvd., Atlanta, Georgia 30312
  P) 404-525-4440 F) 404-525-4545
  www.oasisrecording.com
  bob@oasisrecording.com

- One Star Recording
  5724 Riverdale Rd., Suite C-4, College Park, GA 30349
  P) 678-791-9607

- Orphan Studio
  684 Antone Street, Suite 110, Atlanta, Georgia 30318
  P) 404-352-0666 F) 404-351-7775
  www.orphanstudio.com
  glenn@orphanstudio.com

- Paradise Recording Studio
  1651 Link Overlook, Atlanta, GA 30088
  P) 404-351-0086
  Paradise1651@aol.com

- Patchwerk Recording Studios
  1094 Hemphill, Atlanta, GA 30318
  P) 404-874-9880 F) 404-874-9834
  www.patchwerk.com

- Platinum Sound Recording Studio
  500-A N. Slappery Blvd., Albany, GA 31701
  P) 229-883-3009

- Power Source Entertainment
  5295 Highway 78, Suite D-359
  Stone Mountain, GA 30087
  P) 404-288-3638 Cell) 404-886-8105
  www.powersource-ent.com

- Pro South Entertainment Recording Studios

3060 Bugle Dr., Duluth, GA 30096
P) 770-455-3828 F) 770-455-3821
www.prosouthentertainment.com
info@prosouthentertainment.com

- Red Reign Entertainment
  2579 Park Central Boulevard, Decatur, GA 30035
  P) 678-418-5144
  www.redreignstudios.com
  kecia@redreignstudios.com

- Red Swan Studio
  5658 Riverdale Rd., Unit-Q, College Park, GA 30349
  P) 770-909-9779

- Rex Trax Inc.
  1255 Buford Hwy., Suite 206, Suwanee, GA 30024
  P) 678-730-0008 F) 678.868.1247
  www.rextrax.com
  service@rextrax.com

- Rockstudio
  1409 Newcastle St., Brunswick, GA 31520
  www.rockstudio.com
  info@rockstudio.com
  P) 912 280-0227

- Shangri-La Recordings
  1456 Boulevard SE, Atlanta, GA 30315
  P) 404-624-4092 F) 404-624-4045
  www.shangri-lastudios.com
  music@shangri-lastudios.com

- Silent Sound Studios
  588 Trabert Ave., Atlanta, GA 30309
  P) 404-350-9199 F) 404-350-9562

- Sonica
  500 Bishop Street, Suite C-2, Atlanta, GA 30318
  P) 404-350-9540 F) 404-350-9439
  www.sonicarecording.com
  john@sonicarecording.com steve@sonicarecording.com

- Sound Decision Studios
  P.O. Box 4141, Duluth, GA 30096
  P) 770-813-1870
  www.sounddecisionstudios.com
  bstephens@sounddecisionstudios.com

- Sound Level Recording
  6181 Memorial Drive #A, Stone Mountain, GA 30083
  P) 770-469-2021
  www.soundlevelstudio.com
  info@soundlevelstudio.com

- Sound Master Recording Studio
  P.O. Box K, Alma, GA, 31510
  P) 912-632-0244 F) 912-632-0703
  www.soundmasterstudio.com

- Southern Tracks Recording
  3051 Clairmont Rd., NE, Atlanta, GA 30329
  P) 404-329-0147 F) 404-329-0162
  www.southerntracks.com
  mike@southerntracks.com

- Studio 35
  134 South Clayton St., Lawrenceville, GA 30045
  P) 770-338-5733

- Syncrecy Recordings
  P.O. Box 742, Atlanta, GA 30019
  P) 678-377-8892
  www.syncrecy.com
  syncrecy@aol.com

- The Odyssey Studio
  198 N. First Street, Colbert, GA 30628
  P) 706-540-1076 F) 706-613-3545
  www.theodysseystudio.com
  P_Rives@TheOdysseyStudio.com

- The Sound Lab
  2652 S. Cobb Dr., Suite C, Smyrna, GA 30080
  P) 770-803-0014 F) 770-803-9198 Cell) 678-520-5373
  www.soundlabstudio.com

info@soundlabstudio.com or thesoundlab@earthlink.net

- Trac City Entertainment
  Greenbriar Marketplace
  2975 Headland Dr., Booth D-6, Atlanta, GA 30311
  P) 678-904-7905 Cell) 770-256-5409

- Tree Sound Studios
  4610 Peachtree Industrial Blvd., Norcross GA 30071
  P) 770-242-8944 F) 770-242-0155
  www.treesoundstudios.com
  nina@treesoundstudios.com

- Twelve Oak Studios
  620 Powder Springs St., Smyrna, GA 30080
  P) 770-435-2220

- Upper Room Studios
  403 Reagan Rd., Rebecca, GA 31783
  P) 229-831-7585
  www.upperroomrecording.com
  greg@upperroomrecording.com

- Venusian Music Studio
  P.O. Box 46502, Lawrenceville, GA 30044
  P) 404-840-7574
  www.venusianmusicstudio.com
  info@vnusianmusicstudio.com

- Wet Basement Studios
  225 Corinth Ct., Roswell, GA 30075
  P) 770-993-8074 F) 770-993-4961
  www.wetbasement.com
  lynn@wetbasement.com

- Whippoorwill Sound
  2878 Jonquil Drive, Smyrna, Georgia 30080
  P) 770-333-9372
  www.atlantastudio.com
  wilhodge@mindspring.com

- White Dog Studios
  800 Forrest St. N.W. Atlanta GA 30318
  P) 404-355-2200 F) 404-355-2204
  www.whitedogstudios.net
  info@whitedogstudios.net

- Wonder Dog Sounds
  920 Roxton Cir., Marietta, GA 30064
  P) 770-693-3954
  www.wonderdogsounds.com

- Writeside Productions
  327 Buckingham Drive, Marietta GA 30066
  P) 770-928-1955
  www.writeside.biz
  david@writeside.biz

- ZAC-Zumpano Recording Complex
  669 Antone Street NW, Atlanta, GA 30318
  P) 404-603-8040 F) 404-603-8010
  www.zacrecording.com
  info@zacrecording.com

Where may I get a U.P.C. Barcode?

- U.C.C. - Uniform Code Council
  Customer Service 7887
  Washington Village Dr., Suite 300, Dayton, OH 45459
  P) 937-435-3870 F) 937-435-7317
  www.uc-council.org
  info@uc-council.org

How may I get a parental advisory label?

The industry standard parental advisory label that is placed on CDs may be obtained through the RIAA (Recording Industry Association of America). The Parental Advisory Label normally is put on music sold at retail stores that has questionable and/or potentially offensive language.

How do I contact the RIAA?

- RIAA-Recording Industry Association of America
  1330 Connecticut Avenue, Suite 300
  Washington D.C. 20036
  P) 202-775-0101 F) 202-775-7253
  www.riaa.com
  webmaster@riaa.com

CD/DVD/VINYL MANUFACTURERS

You will need to consider set-up prices, over & under run charges, turnaround time, taxes, shipping/handling and hidden cost before getting your CD or Vinyl pressed.

Set-up prices vary from company to company and project to project, but normally are associated with any first printing project. For instance, there was a set-up cost of like $100 for a CD release I had several years ago. After your first printing there usually is no more set-up fee. Of course, if you change something on the CD or insert then you will be subject to a new set-up fee.

To ensure that the price you are quoted is the price that you pay for duplication, always ask at the end of your conversation with the manufacturer "are there any other fees that I need to be aware of? For example, does the price you just quoted me include taxes, shipping/handling and/or any other fees that we haven't talked about? This will ensure you pay the price you are quoted and not a penny more. Tell them JaWar, author of the Atlanta Music Industry Connection Book sent you!

- A Black Clan Distribution & Manufacturing Inc.
  P) 877-706-7316 P) 770-907-8665 F) 770-907-9216

www.ablackclan.com
juan@ablackclan.com

- Atlanta Manufacturing Group
  83 Walton St., Third Floor, Atlanta, GA 30303
  P) 404-230-9559 F) 230-9558
  www.amgcds.com
  info@amgcds.com

- Creative Media
  2783 Senecca Trail, Duluth, GA 30096-6298
  P) 770-447-8137
  www.creativemedia.com
  sales@creativemedia.com

- HT Media
  P.O. Box 1295, Lithonia, GA 30058
  P) 770-987-9200 F) 770-987-2385
  ht_media@hotmail.com

- Kopy Katz Duplication
  2432 Brantley St., Atlanta, GA 30318
  P) 404-806-7495
  www.kopykatzduplikation.com
  munigraphics@comcast.net

- MDS
  824-B Memorial Dr., Atlanta, GA 30316
  P) 404-584-0372 F) 404-584-9406
  www.mdsinconline.com

- Mindzai
  1139 Euclid Avenue, Atlanta, GA 30307
  P) 404-577-8484 F) 404-577-5895
  www.mindzai.net

- New World Group
  1136 Crescent Ave., Suite 12, Atlanta, GA 30309
  P) 404-885-9890 F) 404-885-9971
  www.newworldmultmedia.net

- ON4 Productions
  684 Antone St., NW Suite 110, Atlanta, GA 30318

P) 888-710-5157 P) 404-603-9900 F) 404-351-7775
www.on4prod.com

- Project 70 Audio Services
  433 Bishop St., NW Suite CD, Atlanta, GA 30310
  P) 404-875-7000 F) 404-875-7007
  www.project70.com

- Quick Media
  981 Joseph E. Lowery Blvd. Ste 100, Atlanta, GA 30318
  P) 404-685-8718 F) 404-685-8711
  www.quickmediallc.com

- Straight from the Soul
  5741 Wells Circle, Stone Mountain, GA 30087
  P) 770-413-2464
  straightent@aol.com

- Tape Warehouse
  2688 Peachtree Sq., Doraville, GA 30360
  P) 770-458-1679 F) 770-458-0276
  www.tapewarehouse.com

- Yourmusiconcd.com
  421 A-1 Pike Blvd., Lawrenceville, GA 30045
  P) 877-442-0933 P) 678-442-0933 F) 678-377-9765
  sns@yourmusiconcd.com

PRINTERS FOR FLYERS & CD-INSERTS

Flyers are a cost-effective method for promoting your business or new release and should be considered as one of your promotional tools. One of the best ways to ensure that you maximize your flyers potential is to include as much contact information on the flyer as possible. For instance, include two phone numbers, two emails, a website and a physical mailing address. Your contact details do not have to be BIG, just large enough to be read. Remember, you want to make it easy for people to locate you in the event they want to book your band, hire you to speak, produce a track or provide legal services, etc.

A gentleman contacted me about registering for the next Music Therapy 101 Music Conference. He said he had one of the flyers for about three years and was just now calling. Had I not included a working number on the flyer I would have missed a paying registrant for the upcoming Music Therapy 101 Music Conference.

Some of the places that flyers may be distributed are music and specialty retail stores, music conferences, talent showcases, open-mics, festivals, barbershops, beauty salons, radio stations, high schools and college campuses. While not always practical, it is advisable to get permission before distributing your flyers at any of these locations or events. However, the truth is that sometimes you will have to take the guerilla marketing approach, go in like a Navy Seal, do your work (pass out flyers) and keep it moving.

I have been kicked out of malls, clubs, schools and special events for distributing flyers and selling my CDs, but by the time I was detected the mission had been completed. Of course, I'm not advocating that you do anything illegal or out of good character, but merely sharing my own experience.

One experience in particular proved to be quite the adventure. My group, the Family Tree and our label, Kemetic Records were in Charlotte, NC promoting either the Paranormal Activity or Dark Ages II release, I'm not sure which one. In any event, we went to one of the local malls and started distributing flyers and selling our CDs. This was a new approach for selling CDs in the Charlotte area, so folks were intrigued and very supportive. It didn't take long before mall security and local law enforcement were planning a course of action. Being the vets that we are, the Family Tree and Kemetic Records Promotional Team were well aware of the developments. However, this only motivated us to increase our hand-to-hand sells in a most expedient (faster) manner. We were on the second level when mall security backed by local law enforcement approached us. Before they began to speak to us, we asked for their support in purchasing our new release. This caught security off guard and bought us a few more minutes to sell more CDs to people standing around who wanted to know what was going on. Eventually, security escorted us out of the mall, so we went to a few more malls a repeated the process. By the end of the day, we had accomplished our task given the number of CDs we sold and the amount of flyers that were distributed.

The cost of printing flyers has become very economical over the years. Most printers make their money from design charges, so make sure that you know what you want or you could be paying a pretty penny for your design work. You might find a high school or college student that would design your artwork for exposure sake, versus receiving financial compensation. Essentially, you would offer to print the graphic artist's name, phone number and email on your flyer in exchange for them designing the flyer for you. This would give them a great deal of exposure and build their professional portfolio. In addition, you would receive quality graphic design without paying a great deal of money. It could be a win/win for everyone.

Let people around you know that you are looking for a graphic designer and you will come across someone that may assist you. Tell them JaWar, author of the Atlanta Music Industry Connection Book sent you!

- Ananse Creative
  P) 404-344-9343 P) 678-592-4795
  www.anansecreative.com
  anansecreative@bellsouth.net

- Claxton Printing Co.
  408 Woodward Ave., SE, Atlanta, GA 30312
  P) 404-521-0933 F) 404-688-5446
  www.claxtonprinting.com
  jim@claxtonprinting.com

- Digiprint
  2395 Pleasantdale Rd., Suite 4-B, Atlanta, GA 30340
  P) 770-368-2060 F) 770-368-9943

- DocuGraphix, Inc.
  1646 Collingwood Drive, SE, Marietta, GA 30067
  P) 770-217-3628
  www.docugraphix.com
  customer.service@docugraphix.com

- Envision Printing
  1266 Kennestone Cir, Suite 105, Marietta, GA 30066
  P) 678-355-6748 F) 678-355-6637
  www.envisionprinting.com
  cs@envisionprinting.com

- Extreme Media
  1440 Dutch Valley Pl., Suite 945, Atlanta, GA 30324
  P) 404-815-0553 F) 404-815-0314
  www.extremeatlanta.com

- Gazelle Printing & Consulting
  20 Executive Park Dr., Ste 2002, Atlanta, GA 30329
  P) 404-320-6926 Cell) 404-454-0668 F) 404-320-5450
  www.gazelleprinting.com
  dalegriffin@gazelleprinting.com

- Image Link
  1379 Chattahoochee Ave., Atlanta, GA 30318
  P) 404-605-0400 F) 404-605-0464
  www.imagelink.net
  staff2@imagelink.net

- Industry Outlet
  684 Antone St. Suite 105, Atlanta, GA 30318
  P) 404-417-9777 P) 877-417-9777 F) 404-759-2072
  print@theindustryoutlet.com

- Inkling Print and Design
  2483 E Briarcliff Rd., Atlanta, GA 30329
  P) 678-388-9662 F) 404-759-2154
  www.inklingprint.com
  info@inklingprint.com

- Kudzu Graphics
  1835 MacArthur Blvd., Atlanta, GA 30318
  P) 404-350-9776 F) 404-684-9554
  www.kudzugraphics.com

- Small Business Promotions, Inc.
  P.O. Box 1348, Redan, GA 30074
  P) 678-886-8792 P) 770-557-0938
  www.designsnprint.com
  orders@designsnprint.com

- Star Shooters
  277-B East Paces Ferry Rd, Atlanta, GA 30305
  P) 404-869-8844 F) 404-869-8833

- Southern Stamp & Stencil
  428 Edgewood Ave., Atlanta, GA 30312
  P) 800-241-0985 P) 404-522-4431 F) 404-522-4507
  www.southernstamp.com
  info@southernstamp.com

DIGITAL DISTRIBUTION COMPANIES

Digital distribution should be included in your business, marketing and overall strategic planning. Digital distribution affords you the opportunity to tap into a worldwide market 24 hours a day, 7 days a week. In addition, digital distribution creates opportunities, whereby you may receive passive income and stay in direct contact with current and potential fans and business associates.

Passive income is where you get paid royalties (money) long after the initial work has been completed. For example, if you record a song in 2006 and the song continues to sale in 2030 with little to no effort on your part then you have created a passive income opportunity for yourself.

The passive income opportunity is real, especially if you create and control your own copyrights and music publishing. Let's say that you made a song you created in

2006 available for sale via a digital download on 10 websites, where you received a $.50 cent royalty each time the song was downloaded. In addition, let's assume that you have been promoting very well and each site gets 100 downloads a month. You would effectively receive $500 a month in royalties. Here is how the math (money) breaks down.

$.50/cent download X 100 downloads month= $50/month
$50/month site X 10 sites = $500/month
$500 X 12/months = $6,000/year

Keep in mind that you still may have to actively promote your music, informing current and potential fans where your music may be purchased. The point here is after you have created a practical plan and executed your plan you should begin to see sales with minimum effort on your part. This will afford you greater control over your time to enjoy life, help the less fortunate and leave a growing financial empire to your children or charity of your choice. As time progresses you should continue to follow a system that will create opportunities for you to generate passive or residual royalties (income). Remember digital distribution may include downloadable music or streaming audio files via the Internet, ringtones and a number of other applications yet to be created.

Below is a list of digital distribution companies. Visit the sites and work with the ones that are best suited for you. Please let me know about your continued success by e-mailing me at jawar@mt101.com.

- http://ci-info.com/dcm.html
- www.101distribution.com
- www.7digitalmedia.com
- www.audiolunchbox.com
- www.awal.co.uk
- www.buyindiemusic.com
- www.buythiscd.com

- www.catchmusic.net
- www.cdbaby.com
- www.cdbrainstorm.com
- www.cdfreedom.com
- www.cdpimp.com
- www.cdstreet.com
- www.digitalmusicworksinc.com
- www.digitalrightsagency.com
- www.easybe.com
- www.galaxydiscs.com
- www.groupietunes.com
- www.indiegate.com
- www.indypendence.com
- www.iodalliance.com
- www.irisdistribution.com
- www.isound.com
- www.jivjiv.com
- www.lightningcd.com
- www.listentomydemo.com
- www.mperia.com
- www.musicfist.com
- www.onlineradiopromotion.com
- www.rapstation.com
- www.rightsrouter.com
- www.soundclick.com
- www.streetcds.com
- www.theorchard.com
- www.ugscienc.com
- www.unlimitedtracks.com
- www.unpluggednetwork.com
- www.vitaluk.com
- www.weedshare.com
- www.xingtone.com

DISTRIBUTION COMPANIES

Many artists think that getting distribution is the end all be all state to advancing their music careers. However, getting distribution is not really the difficult task. The difficulty comes in encouraging (getting) the buying public to go into the store and purchase your music. Before seeking distribution you should create a demand for your music at the retail level. This will include building a strong street buzz, actively promoting your live performances, getting interviews and CD reviews from print and on-line media sources and growing a fan base mailing list. I go over this in greater detail in the How to Market & Promote Your Independent Release section.

While creating a buzz you will want to find out who the buyer is for your style or genre of music at the distribution companies. Invite the buyer to a business breakfast, lunch or dinner in an effort to build a relationship with them. It is customary for the person asking for a business breakfast, lunch or dinner meeting to pay the bill, so prepare to do so and tip the waiter or waitress well. This meeting is considered a business meeting and should be tax-deductible. Of course, you will want to check with your tax professional i.e. C.P.A. (Certified Public Account) to be sure.

Have specific questions to ask the buyer about the traditional distribution process. Ask what they are seeking from an artist or independent label. Allow them to guide you through the process. This is the point were you want to ask questions and listen. I guarantee you if you listen, you will learn most valuable information.

In addition to inviting the decision maker at the distribution company to a business luncheon, you will want to invite them to your live performance. However, only do this when you have a consistent substantial following that are buying your music at your shows. This will allow the buyer to see that you have built a buzz for yourself. More importantly, they will see that you have created a demand for your product. Tell them JaWar, author of the Atlanta Music Industry Connection Book sent you!

- IMD-International Music Distribution
  764 Glenshire Ct., Riverdale, GA 30274
  P) 770-909-7427 F) 770-909-7756
  bradimd@bellsouth.net

- MDI Distribution
  P.O. Box 2738, Tybee Island, GA 31328
  P) 404.806.0388 P) 800-898-7812 F) 404-806-0387
  www.mdidistribution.com
  info@mididistribution.com

- New Leaf Distribution Company
  401 Thornton Rd, Lithia Springs, GA 30122
  P) 770-948-7845 F) 770-944-2313
  www.newleaf-dist.com

- Red Distribution
  2531 Briarcliff Rd., NE, Atlanta, GA
  www.redmusic.com
  P) 404-679-6084

- Select-O-Hits Distribution
  1981 Fletcher Creek Dr., Memphis, TN 38133
  P) 901-388-1190
  www.selectohits.com

- Southern Music Distribution
  P.O. Box 921969, Norcross, GA 30010
  P) 770-447-5159 F) 770-449-9337
  www.southernmusicdigital.com

- **UPD-U Pressing & Distribution**
  233 Mitchell St., Ste 320 Atlanta, GA 30303
  P) 404-454-1091
  www.updonline.com
  updonline@yahoo.com

GETTING YOUR OWN WEBSITE

There is no excuse for not having a website if you are serious about building a successful career in the music business. A website should be included in your business, marketing and strategic plans. A few steps toward creating an on-line presence includes creating a domain (website) name that is easy to remember, relates to you or your business and registering that domain name. In addition, a great website will not have any numbers or hyphens in it.

There are a number of sites like cdbaby.com that allow you to create an on-line presence through their domain. While this should be utilized, at the end of the day you will want and need to have your own website address, such as www.mt101.com. You may want to have your site designed by www.websitesatl.com Below are a few sites where you may register your domain name:

- www.buydomains.com
- www.myrealebiz.com
- www.networksolutions.com
- www.omnis.com
- www.yahoo.com

PHOTOGRAPHERS

- Arial Productions
  2404 Huntingdon Chase, Atlanta, GA 30350
  P) 770-394-9392 F) 404-394-8285
  greggcoyle2000@yahoo.com

- D&G Enterprise
  P.O. Box 49692, Atlanta, GA 30329
  P) 404-633-6825
  www.dandgenterprise.biz
  l_dear@dandgenterprise.biz

- D2K Models Design Group
  2230 Leicester Way, Atlanta, GA 30316

P) 404-441-5794
www.d2kmodels.com
moussa@d2kmodels.com

- Diamond Photography
  P.O. Box 638, Redan, GA 30074
  P) 770-354-6378
  www.theultimatediamondmine.com

- Foto Illusion Studios
  2275 Northwest Parkway, Suite 115 Marietta, GA 30067
  P) 678-990-5211
  www.fotoillusion.com

- JWJ Photography
  2975 Headland Dr., Atlanta, GA 30331
  P) 404-783-0041

- Kenny's Photography
  1729 Rogers Ave. SW, Atlanta, GA 30310
  P) 404-758-7301 Cell) 404-247-2018

- Laser Photographics
  290 Hilderbrand Dr., Suite B-9, Atlanta, GA 30328
  P) 404-531-0555 F) 404-531-0044
  www.laserphotographics.com
  laserphotgraphics@mindsping.com

- Photomax
  3375 Buford Hwy, Suite 1020, Atlanta, GA 30329
  P) 404-320-1494 F) 404-320-6291
  www.photomax1hr.com
  photomax@aol.com

- Primetime
  P.O. Box 49531, Atlanta, GA 30359
  P) 404-731-2343
  www.primetimeatlanta.com

- Sean Cokes Photography
  650 Hamilton Ave., Studio Z, Atlanta, GA 30312
  P) 404-622-7733
  www.seancokes.com

scokesphoto@yahoo.com

- Holidayshots Photography
  3535 Peachtree Rd., Suite 520-151, Atlanta, GA 30326
  P) 404-518-0990
  www.holidayshots.com
  photographer@holidayshots.com

- Tshanti Photography Studio
  300 MLK Jr. Dr., SE #144, Atlanta, GA 30312
  P) 678-768-4647
  tshantphoto@hotmail.com

- Upscale Images
  P.O. 2585, Decatur, GA 30031
  P) 770-496-4393 Cell) 678-592-0129
  www.upscale-images.com
  upscale_images@msn.com

MUSIC CONFERENCES

Music conferences are a fantastic way to network, negotiate and know the business of music. By attending a music conference you have the ability to create windows of opportunity for yourself. This is achieved by having a clearly identifiable goal. For instance, your goal may be to network with a Kemetic Records Representative or to gather contact information from other industry professionals. Music conferences may also be used to negotiate deals. For example, a conference may be a great time to discuss in greater detail a project that you are working on with another industry professional. To make the best use of your time, contact the person you intend on meeting with prior to the conference, set an itinerary, a time and meeting location. This ensures that you both know what to expect from the meeting and that time is scheduled to accomplish the task.

With practical planning you will find that music conferences are a fantastic way to network, negotiate and know the business of music.

Before attending two music conferences I set measurable goals & objectives. My goals & objectives where to distribute flyers to everyone at the conferences, to get as many emails as possible, to distribute as many copies of the Atlanta Music Industry Connection Book as possible, to have fun, as well as brand myself and company. As the conferences came to an end and people started saying, "you gave me that flyer already" I knew I had achieved my first goal. In addition, I had a bag full of business cards, flyers and CDs with e-mail addresses that let me know I had come very close to achieving my second goal. Also, my inventory of books started to dwindle, that indicated that I was almost home free with accomplishing my goals and objectives. Last, I met a lot people who were excited about their music careers and we often made fun of paying dues in the industry, so I laughed a lot. In short: I had fun and was home free! You see I had accomplished my goals and objectives at both conferences.

I have found that when I set realistic goals and write them down or record them in my PDA, I tend to accomplish them and my experience at any given music industry conference (like Music Therapy 101) is worth my time and effort. There are a number of music conferences, talent showcases, open-mics and music industry networking activities that you may attend. To ensure you maximize your opportunities, set measurable goals and objectives.

Below is a list of music conferences to consider attending. Let them know you found them in the Atlanta Music Industry Connection Book by JaWar.

- A&R Music1.com, LLC.
  2280 Wren Rd., SE, Suite 521, Conyers, GA 30094
  P) 770-686-9100
  www.armusic1.com

- Atlantis Music Conference
  1339 Canton Rd., Suite E, Marietta, GA 30066
  P) 770-499-8600 F) 770-499-8650
  www.atlantismusic.com

- Future Stars Music Conference
  1646 Collingwood Drive, SE, Marietta, Georgia 30067
  P) 770-217-3762
  www.futurestarsmusicconference.com
  info@futurestarsmusicconference.com

- Million Dollar Record Pool Conference
  2459 Roosevelt Hwy. Suite B-1, College Park GA 30337
  P) 404-766-1275 F) 404.559.0117
  http://mildol.com
  mde@mildol.com

- **MUSIC THERAPY 101**
  P.O. Box 52682, Atlanta, GA 30355
  P) 800-963-0949
  www.mt101.com
  questions@mt101.com

- Southeast Urban Music Conference
  P.O. Box 670296, Marietta, GA 30066
  P) 770-621-5820 F) 770-973-0136
  www.smiurban.com
  smiurban@comcast.net

How do I find more shows to perform in?

Ask other bands/artists where they perform and how they hear about new opportunities. This allows you to benefit from someone else's knowledge very fast. Likewise, you should share your information with other artist.

Networking is your key to success here. What this means is that you want to ask everyone that you know related to the music industry if they are aware of places where you may perform. For example, ask folks that work at music retail stores, studio engineers, party/club promoters, DJs, music publicists, booking agents, record company executives and entertainment attorneys. Letting the right people know you are ready and willing to perform is a step in the right direction to finding more places to showcase your talent. Another way to showcase your talent is to create your own show. Pursue local publications such as

Rolling Out Weekly and Creative Loafing Newspapers, as there are often announcements for talent shows and open-mics.

REMEMBER TO:

- Ask other artists where they perform.
- Ask music industry professionals if they know of places for you to perform.
- Read Rolling Out Weekly & Creative Loafing for Talent Showcase Announcements.
- Create your own venue for performing.

TALENT SHOW/OPEN MIC ORGANIZERS

Performing in front of A&R and other music industry professionals should not be your sole purpose for showcasing your talent on stage. If executed properly, whether you perform in front of 1 person or 1,000 people, you can optimize your live performance experience to improve your craft, increase your fan base, generate sales and above all else have fun!

First, practice, practice, practice before you set foot on stage. This will build your confidence while on stage. Furthermore, you will demonstrate that you are serious about your craft. Second, know that every performance is more mental than physical. So, prepare yourself as though your next performance is in front of loyal fans that have paid hard earned money to see you perform. Third, get someone to video tape all of your performances. This way you can go back and review your show. Keep in mind that other bands, speakers and athletic teams do this to improve their craft. In addition, at some point in your career you may be able to professionally package and sell the footage. Fourth, designate someone to get contact names, physical & email addresses and phone numbers of everyone at your performance. By doing so you can invite those same people to your next performance. When your

CDs and t-shirts are ready you will have a potential client base interested in supporting you. While these steps just touch the surface of using live performances to improve your craft, increase your fan base, generate sales and have fun while on stage this should give you an idea as to how you may best utilize your talent, no matter the size of the audience. Below is a list of companies that produce regular events for artists to showcase their skills and abilities:

- A&J Connection
  P) 770-981-5114
  ajsconn@bellsouth.net

- Dreamcatchers Entertainment
  P.O. Box 262, Stone Mountain, GA, 30086
  P) 404-454-4200
  bme2k3@hotmail.com

- HU Party Productions
  P.O. Box 55044, Atlanta, GA 30308
  P) 404-484-0433
  www.huparty.com
  info@huparty.com

- I am a Star
  4591 Rockbridge Rd, Stone Mountain, GA 30083
  P) 800-632-5137
  www.iamastarr.com
  info@iamastarr.com

- Lady Di/Bar Red Entertainment Group
  P.O. Box 281, Rex, GA 30273
  P) 770-912-8065 P) 770-931-2945 F) 770-931-2226
  www.ldbr-entgrp.com
  info@ldbr-entgrp.com

- MIC Club
  5147 Fair Forest Dr., Ste 4 Stone Mountain, GA 30088
  www.4kingsent.com
  info@4kingsent.com

- NextUp Entertainment
  2867 Hillwood Rd., Suite #6, Atlanta, GA 30319
  P) 404-964-5910
  www.nextupent.com
  jagwonder@yahoo.com

- Open Mic Entertainment
  P) 770-864-7811
  dcraver@openmic.us

- Red Light Café
  553 Amsterdam Ave., Atlanta, GA 30306
  P) 404-874-7828
  www.redlightcafe.com

- Taylord Entertainment
  4600 East Ponce De Leon, Ste 406 Clarkston, GA 30021
  P) 770-482-8797
  www.tay-lordentertainment.com

- US Entertainment
  4292 Trotters Way Dr., Snellville, GA 30039
  P) 678-887-6876
  www.usentertainment.8m.com
  mrgresham@usentertainment.8m.com

CREATING YOUR OWN TALENT-SHOW

Creating your own live performance opportunity may be one of the best ways to increase awareness of your band or group. One of the best ways of putting on a successful show is to study those that do it and implement the great things they do and improve on the others. A few of the basics you will need to consider before producing a show are:

- The purpose of the show or what you hope to get accomplish or get out of the show
- The target market (demographic)
- The date, venue (location), time of day and ticket price

- A marketing and promotions campaign
- Cost-analysis including break-even point
- Security and staff needed to make the event safe and successful

Music Industry Connection offers one-on-one consultation to assist you in organizing your talent show. To get started give us a call at 800-963-0949 or send an email to questions@mt101.com.

RECORD COMPANIES

- Aarow Records
  5917 Old National Hwy., College Park, GA 30349
  P) 770-210-5708
  www.arrow-records.com

- Air Gospel
  881 Memorial Drive, SE, Atlanta, GA 30316
  P) 404-524-6835 F) 404-681-0033
  www.airgospel.com
  air@airgospel.com

- Ahunit and Fifth Street Entertainment
  889 Gatehouse Dr., Suite-B, Decatur, GA 30032
  P) 404-294-6154 P) 678-613-6469
  patlblkice@aol.com

- ArcTheFinger Records
  1372 Peachtree St., Suite 300, Atlanta, GA 30309
  P) 404-339-0051 Ext. 201 F) 404-339-0061
  www.archthefinger.com
  b@archthefinger.com

- Around The World Records
  P.O. Box 6967, Marietta, GA 30065
  P) 770-565-9455
  www.aroundtheworldrecords.com

- B3 Neighbahood Productions, LLC
  P.O. Box 87435, College Park, GA 30337
  P) 770-873-5364 F) 770-471-0036
  www.b3np.com
  neighbahoodpro@yahoo.com

- Big Cat Records
  500 Bishop St., Suite E5, Atlanta, GA 30318
  P.O. Box 490956, Atlanta, GA 30349
  P) 866-603-8229 F) 404-603-9231
  www.bigcatrecords.net

- Big Oomp Records
  Attn: Store Promotions Dept.

1079 MLK Drive NW, Ste 2, Atlanta, GA 30314
P) 404-758-4210
nakia@bigoomprecords.com

- BME (Black Market Entertainment) Recordings
  2144 Hills Ave., Suite D-2, Atlanta, GA 30318
  P) 404-367-8130 F) 404-367-8630
  www.bmerecordings.com
  dsearch@bmerecordings.com

- Boss Up, Inc
  P.O. Box 310330, Atlanta, GA 31131
  www.bossupbu.com
  bossupinc@comcast.net

- CGI
  Attn: Platinum Entertainment
  11415 Old Roswell Rd., Alpharetta, GA 30004
  P) 770-664-9262 F) 770-664-7316

- Deep End Records
  3469 Lawrencville Hwy., Suite 304, Tucker, GA 30084
  P) 678-280-0295 F) 770-908-8798
  www.deepend-records.com

- Division 1 Entertainment
  P.O. Box 82873, Hapeville, GA 30354
  P) 678-559-5994 P) 404-918-0790
  www.division1ent.com

- Dollyhood Records
  4546 Columbus Rd., Macon, GA 31206
  P) 478-477-9900 F) 478-477-7030
  dollyhoodrecord@aol.com

- DTP-Disturbing the Peace
  1451 Wood Mount LN., Atlanta, GA 30318
  P) 404-351-7387

- East End Records of Atlanta
  P.O. Box 1968, Woodstock, GA 30188
  P) 770-924-9405
  www.eastendrecords.net

- EWS Enterprises
  P.O. Box 360726, Decatur, GA 30036
  P) 404-289-7194
  www.ewaltersmith.com

- Grand Hustle Entertainment
  147 Walker St., Atlanta, GA 30313
  P) 404-522-8383 P) 404-456-1778
  www.grandhustle.com

- Immortalized Entertainment
  P.O. Box 1079, Atlanta, GA 30301
  P) 770-377-7553
  www.immortalizedentertainment.com
  immortalizedent@aol.com

- Interscope/Geffen/A&M
  400 Interstate North Pkwy, Ste 450, Atlanta, GA 30339
  P) 678-742-9016 F) 678-742-9087
  www.umusic.com

- Invisible Records
  1118 10th Ave., Columbus, GA 31901
  P) 706-660-1555 F) 706-660-1537
  www.invisible-records.com
  info@invisible-records.com

- Jive Records
  1000 Abernathy Road Suite 200, Atlanta, GA 30328
  P) 770-673-5850
  www.jiverecords.com

- **KEMETIC RECORDS**
  P.O. Box 52682, Atlanta, GA 30355
  www.kemetic.com

- LaVista Records
  P.O. Box 676, Woodstock, GA 30188
  P) 678-494-1091 F) 678-494-1091
  www.lavistarecords.com
  pius@lavistarecords.com

- Livewire Recordings
  3050 Royal Blvd. South, Ste 110, Alpharetta, GA 30022
  P) 678-624-1770 F) 678-624-1774
  www.livewirerecordings.net
  info@livewirerecordings.net

- Modest Music
  P.O. Box 13135, Atlanta, GA 30324
  P) 404-966-5171
  inobe@inobe.net

- Money Makers Records
  3500 Lenox Rd., Suite 1500, Atlanta, GA 30326
  P) 404-819-7186

- Move The Crowd Records, Inc.
  P.O. Box 831822, Stone Mountain, Georgia 30083
  P) 404-866-3780
  www.movethecrowdrecords.com
  info@movethecrowd.com

- N-terface Records
  6750 Peachtree Industrial Blvd., #1703
  Atlanta, GA 30360
  P) 770-263-8575
  www.n-terfacerecords.com
  n-tercacerecords@comcast.com

- NME Records
  Midtown Proscenium Center
  1170 Peachtree St., Suite 1200, Atlanta, GA 30309
  P) 404-885-5754 F) 404-885-5764
  www.nmerecords.com

- Real Deal Records
  794 Evander Holyfield Hwy, Fairburn, GA 30212
  P) 678-817-0766 P) 678-817-0295
  www.realdealrecords.com

- Real Life Records
  220 Timberland Tr., Riverdale, GA 30274
  P) 770-477-5505

- Platinum Rush Music LLC
  889 Gatehouse Dr., B, Decatur , GA 30032
  P) 404-294-6154
  www.platinumrushmusic.com
  patlblkice@aol.com

- Platinum Records
  3695 Cascade Rd F190, Atlanta, GA 30331
  P) 404-344-8238 F) 404-349-4544
  www.realplatinumrecords.com
  info@realplatinumrecords.com

- Purple Ribbon
  684 Antone St., Suite 100 Atlanta, GA 30318
  P) 404-350-3332

- Selsum Records
  401 East Lake Dr., Marietta, GA 30062
  P) 678-560-1067
  selsumrecords1@aol.com

- Shut Eye Records & Agency
  1526 DeKalb Ave., Suite 21, Atlanta, GA 30307
  P) 678-986-5110 F) 404-584-5171
  www.shuteyerecords.com
  hello@shuteyerecords.com

- Sierra-Pearl Records
  P.O. Box 2417 Jonesboro, GA 30237-2417
  Phone & Fax) 678-610-6586
  www.johnnymo.info
  sierrapearl@hotmail.com

- Slam Jamz 2
  7139 Hwy 85, Suite 293, Riverdale, GA 30274
  P) 770-997-9124

- So So Def Recordings Inc.
  1350 Spring St., Suite 700, Atlanta, GA 30309
  P) 404-888-9900 F) 404-888-9901
  www.sosodef.com

- Thrilla Time Records

P.O. Box 102, Union City, GA 30291
P) 404-379-9638 P) 404-336-2182
www.thrillatime.com
thrillatime@thrillatime.com

- Tight 2 Def Records
  580 Stoneglen Chase Dr., Atlanta, GA 30331
  P) 678-508-3897 F) 404-494-3239
  www.tight2defrecords.com
  rah4life@bellsouth.net

- Triad Records
  6350 McDonough Dr., Ste A, Norcross, GA 30093
  P) 770-840-0608 F) 770-446-2036

- Trump Tight Records
  P.O. Box 861, Scottsdale, GA 30079
  P) 404-830-3498

- Tyziq Life Music
  P.O. Box 4333, Marietta, GA 30061
  P) 770-419-3783
  www.touie.net
  2focused@touie.net

- Volume Records, Inc.
  4273 Chamblee Tucker Road, Atlanta, GA 30340
  P) 770-939-8011 F) 770-939-0695
  www.volumerecordsinc.com
  vrinfo@volumerecordsinc.com

- WEA-Warner/Elektra/Atlantic
  817 West Peachtree Street #300, Atlanta, GA 30308
  P) 404-602-3406 F) 404-602-3362

How to Market Your Independent Release

A practical plan, a passion to succeed and a willingness to innovate are most important in marketing your independent release. Make sure your product stands the test of time. In short: your music should be **HOT!**

Make a list of music retail stores, night clubs, colleges & universities, high schools, coffee houses, malls, college, community radio stations, college & high school papers and local magazines. The list of venues and locations should be within an hour of your home market. This will give you the opportunity to penetrate your core market and build a solid fan-base. This is especially, important for the independent label and artist who count on selling CDs, merchandise and tickets to live performances to pay the mortgage.

The next step is to obtain the physical and email addresses, phone and fax numbers of each location mentioned. Begin contacting the colleges and high schools that have newspapers. The goal is to get the music and/or entertainment writer to either interview you and/or write a review of your HOT Music. The writers should receive your type written bio, an 8x10 black & white glossy photo and professionally recorded CD. However, always correspond with the music reviewer before submitting your materials, as some writers may have special requirements. For instance, they may accept a black & white 4x6 photo versus an 8x10 black & white glossy. In addition, you may find that when dealing with commercial publications or publications for profit, that you will be able to secure a positive review once you have placed an ad with that particular magazine or newspaper. While all publications do not require you to place an ad before they will write a review, some do, so artist beware. Before your jaws drop

48

consider the following. Most publications for profit make their money from advertising dollars. Since a review of your music brings awareness to you as an artist and your new release, the magazine is helping you gain greater exposure, which may lead to increased CD sales and attendance at your live performances. Hence, some magazines require that you spend advertising dollars before they will write a review of your music worth reading. In turn you receive a review and the magazine will receive advertising dollars; it is a mutually beneficial opportunity.

You should be simultaneously getting music reviews and working on performing live. When you are beginning your career, you will want to focus on perfecting your craft and building a loyal fan base. This is achieved through performing live at every venue possible. If the opportunity presents itself for you to perform in front of 1,000 people do it. Likewise if the opportunity presents itself for you to perform in front of 10 people, do it. The goal is the same, perfecting your craft and building a loyal fan base. With that said here are some ways to make the most out of your live performances. Invite every person on your contact hit list to your live performances. Yes, music writers, DJ's, music retail store managers, club owners, record pool directors, etc. Remember your goal is to get your music heard by potential fans that will buy future releases, your merchandise and support your concerts. One way to get people to try something new is by offering a discount. For example, you may want to sell your full length CD for $7. Some companies have been extremely successful at selling more products by lowering their prices.

By following these simple steps you may turn a live performance into a window of opportunity, begin building a loyal fan base and sell more music and merchandise. Before each performance designate someone (a group member, manager, brother, sister, husband, wife, etc.) to collect names, phone numbers and email addresses of potential fans. Ensure that your representative has the tools necessary for success. For instance, they should have a preprinted mailing list sheet, ink pen, CDs and merchandise to sell as well. Your retail ready CDs should be priced to sell. For instance, your CD should sell a few dollars less than a national recording artist. Therefore, if a Jay-Z or Jill Scott CD sells for $13.99 you may want to sell your music for $9.99. If you did not use any of your money to press your retail ready CDs you can sell your music for much less and still make a profit. Yes, you can **press 1,000 retail ready CDs without using your own money**, but that jewel is reserved for attendees of my dynamic workshop "How to Market & Promote 1,000 Retail Ready CDs Without Using Your Own Money." For dates, times and locations of future seminars visit **www.mt101.com or call 800-963-0949.**

When do I need a manager?

That depends on your personality and business savvy. For instance, some people have a knack for networking, are extremely organized, knowledgeable about the music business and do well in improving and perfecting their craft. So, in the beginning of your career you may not need the service of a manager. However, as you become more commercially successful and are asked to make guest appearances, sought after for endorsements and perform more extensively, you may seek the services of a qualified manager who would help you navigate your growing success.

However, you may need the services of a manager in the early stages of your career to help you identify career goals and objectives, develop your craft, network with music industry professionals and focus on achieving success.

How should I select a qualified manager?

While there are a number of factors that you should consider before choosing a manager a few include the manager's **ability to multi-task, organizational skills,** professionalism, knowledge of the business of music, extensive industry contact list and believe in you as an artist. In addition, the manager should have some knowledge of contract negotiations, how record companies operate and basic bookkeeping and/or accounting skills.

When do I need an entertainment attorney?

As an artist you should seek a qualified music attorney before signing any contracts. In many cases if you are a less seasoned or business savvy artist you may also seek a qualified entertainment attorney to help negotiate agreements on your behalf.

How should I select an entertainment attorney?

That depends on what you hire the attorney to do and your career goals and objectives. As an artist you may need contract drafting and negotiation, professional career development and/or contacts to decision makers at record companies, publishing companies and T.V. & film studios, etc. Different entertainment attorneys may provide one or all of these services. Some practical factors to consider before selecting a entertainment attorney include:

- How you met the attorney i.e. where they referred to you by a reliable source
- The attorneys experience in the music industry
- Your first instinct (gut feeling) about the attorney (which is probably one of the most important factors of selecting an attorney)
- How much the attorney charges for his/her services and the connections the attorney has in the music business.

Of course, there are other factors that should be considered before selecting which attorney you will hire to work for you, but this should get you started when the time is right.

How much do attorney fees cost?

You can expect to pay anywhere from $150/hr to $300/hr for attorney fees. Like many things in life, an attorney's fees are negotiable. It has been my experience that many attorneys are willing to work with aspiring songwriters and recording artist, if they see that you are serious about your craft and are willing to stay the course. Remember that these attorneys know that you may be the next Jay-Z, Kid Rock, Alicia Keys, Creed, etc. and want the opportunity to represent you. In addition, many of the attorneys had to sacrifice to complete their undergrad and law school studies, so they can appreciate the artist who also has a plan and passion to succeed as they did.

Artist's Revenue Streams

- Publishing Royalties
    1. Mechanical Licenses-CD & Record Sales
    2. Synchronization Licenses-Television, film, commercials i.e. jingles & infomercials
    3. Public Performance-radio airplay
    4. Printed Music-lyric or sheet music
    5. Digital Domain-Digital Downloads, Internet Webcasting, Satellite Radio, Pod-casting, etc.
- Touring-concert ticket sales
- Merchandising-t-shirts, hats, shoes, belts, etc. sold at retail stores, concerts, on the Internet, through direct mail and catalog sales
- Guest appearances on other artists songs
- Product and/or service endorsements
- Artists should read the Creating Wealth Section on page 148 to increase their investing knowledge

PRODUCER'S WORKSHOP

What equipment do I need?

Some sound-creating device i.e. a drum machine, drums, keyboard, etc., a amplifier, speakers and recording device. In many instances a computer and the right software may be a substitute for some of the equipment and sounds you will need. Contact some of the music equipment stores in this book to see what they suggest.

How do I insure my equipment?

If you are a homeowner and your equipment is in your house, your equipment should be insured via your homeowners insurance. However, it is always an excellent idea to double-check with your insurance company. If your music equipment is in your apartment, make sure that you have renters insurance to cover the loss in case your equipment is destroyed. Your leasing office may have information on obtaining renter's insurance or you may look for an insurance company in the yellow pages and on-line.

I know of an entertainment attorney that was renting an apartment in Atlanta. Unfortunately, his apartment complex was burned down and all his personal belongings were destroyed. Fortunately, he had renter's insurance and kept photos and receipts for many of his possessions so the insurance company could replace his belongings. No one was hurt in the fire; but only two people including the attorney had renter's insurance. Make sure you insure your music equipment.

In addition, to homeowner's or renter's insurance you may be able to insure your equipment through a music related organization. For instance, through membership in ASCAP, GMIA or NARAS, etc. you may be eligible (qualify) for insurance to cover the loss of your equipment. The companies below specialize in providing insurance for the music industry are listed below. Tell them you found them in the Atlanta Music Industry Connection Book by JaWar.

- Bruner Insurance Agency, Inc.
  3720 Longview Drive, Suite 6, Atlanta, GA 30341
  P) 770-451-3743 F) 770-451-7006

- Music Pro Insurance Agency
  45 Crossways Park Dr., Woodbury, NY 11797
  P) 800-605-3187 F) 888-290-0302
  www.musicproinsurance.com

- Williams, Turner & Mathis, Inc.
  P.O. Box 450289, Atlanta, GA 31145
  P) 770-934-3248 F) 770-934-3248
  www.wtm-insurance.com
  insurance@wtm-insurance.com

- Robertson Taylor
  315 South Beverly Dr., Suite 201
  Beverly Hills, CA 90210
  www.robertson-taylor.com

When do I need an entertainment attorney?

As a music producer you should seek the services of a qualified entertainment attorney before signing any contracts. In addition, your attorney should help advise you on sampling issues, teach you about the business of music and help increase your contact list of other industry professionals that can help advance your career.

RECORDING STUDIOS

As an aspiring music producer you'll want to be able to capture record and perfect your music production skills easily and inexpensively. That means having access to some basic studio equipment were you can record your raw ideas almost instantaneously. For example, it could be 2:00 am and you might be dreaming of a killer base line with a piano and break-beat on top of it. You might have booked a session for next week at the "BIG" studio, but there is no way your going to remember the base line, piano and break-beat by then. The simple solution, have a drum machine, keyboard/synthesizer, sampler, headphones and/or speakers in your house, so that you can capture, record and perfect your music production skills easily and inexpensively.

In addition, to honing your music production skills easily and inexpensively, owning a pre-production studio will prepare you for recording at a larger facility. **As an aspiring music producer, one of the most important things to remember is that you make hit or hot music, not the equipment. The equipment only allows you to express the arrangement of sounds in your mind and soul.**

There is a wide range of "BIG" studios at your disposal. As a rule of thumb, the least amount of surprises you encounter the better off you are when it comes to recording at these facilities. With that in mind, one of the questions you will want to ask is does the price that you are quoted include the studio engineer's price. Sometimes it does sometimes it doesn't, so remember to ask. In addition, many studios offer block (discount) rates when you book (reserve) say 10 or more hours at a time. So, it is to your advantage to block out time to save money. However, if you are not accustomed to recording for 10 hours then this may be a waste of time and money. Studio prices can range from $35/hr to $200/hr. Remember to bring your own CD-Rs and other record-able devices to the studio. The studio will probably have some on hand, but it will cost you a lot more to buy it from the studio than to bring you own. Hey, the studio is a business, so they are going to make every penny they can. In addition, to the cost you want to ask about the experience of the studio engineer that you will work on your project, what style of music does the studio normally record and if possible to ensure that there is great chemistry between you and the engineer. A few factors to consider before choosing a studio to record in are **studio cost, experience of studio engineer, whether the engineer records your style of music often and chemistry between artist, producer & studio engineer.** Purchasing music equipment and paying for studio time is a business expense. Remember to speak with your tax professional about recouping (getting back) some of these monies when filing your taxes. Refer to page ten for a listing of recording studios.

MUSIC EQUIPMENT & GEAR STORES

Music equipment stores are a great place to meet other musicians and industry professionals. Remember that windows of opportunity are created by those who make them.

You may find another musician that will tell you about future open-mics and music industry networking events. Networking is a two-way street, so be prepared to share your industry contacts with fellow musicians.

Many music equipment stores have a designated area were you can post details about your band's performances. Make sure you take advantage of this opportunity by posting your next gig. This is free promotion and you never know who will read this stuff. Many folks in this book were added to the directory because they took the time to post their business card or flyer in a music equipment store. In addition, I have sold books to people that saw an advertisement for my book in a gear store- so it works.

Tape Warehouse is the "one stop shop" for blank media in Atlanta. Everyone- and I mean *everyone*- in the greater Atlanta area has shopped and/or will shop at Tape Warehouse at some point. Tape Warehouse has a bulletin board that allows you to list your company or band for free.

Also, get to know the owners, managers and front line sales associates of the stores as they are often involved with the music industry in more than one way and may be able to help you further your career. Below is a list of stores that you will want to visit. Tell them you found them in the Atlanta Music Industry Connection Book by JaWar.

- Music & Arts
  1537 North East Expressway, Atlanta, GA 30329
  P) 866-826-4676 F) 404-389-0482

- Atlanta Band Centre-S. Dekalb Plaza
  2746 Candler Rd., Decatur, GA 30034
  P) 404-212-0420 F) 404-244-0811
  www.atlantabandcentre.com
  bandcenter2746@yahoo.com

- Atlanta Band Centre-Evanswood Center
  2928-B Evansmill Rd., Lithonia, GA 30058
  P) 678-526-0909
  www.atlantabandcentre.com
  bandcenter2928@yahoo.com

- Atlanta Band Centre
  5219 Memorial Dr., Stone Mountain, GA 30083
  P) 404-477-3786
  www.atlantabandcentre.com
  bandcenter5055@yahoo.com

- Atlanta Discount Music, Inc.
  4934 Peachtree Rd., Chamblee, GA 30341
  P) 770-457-3400 P) 866-322-6220
  www.atlantadiscountmusic.com

- Atlanta Pro Audio
  1776 Northeast Expressway NE, Atlanta, GA 30329

www.atlantaproaudio.net

- Avata Events Group
  471 Glen Iris Dr., Atlanta, GA 30308
  P) 404-589-9450 F) 404-589-9451
  www.avataeventsgroup.com

- Boutique Guitar Exchange
  1530 Dekalb Avenue, NE, Suite C, Atlanta, GA 30307
  P) 404-614-0345
  www.boutiqueguitarexchange.com

- Century Music Center
  4828 Flat Shoals Pkwy., Decatur, GA
  P) 770-808-1991

- Century Music Center
  5561-J Memorial Dr., Stone Mountain, GA
  P) 770-413-1000

- Galaxy Music
  5236 Highway 78, Stone Mountain, GA 30087
  P) 770-879-8381
  www.galaxymusicusa.com
  galaxymzk@aol.com

- Guitar Center Atlanta
  1485 Northeast Expressway, Atlanta, GA 30329
  P) 404-320-7253 F) 404-633-2522
  www.guitarcenter.com

- Guitar Center Lawrenceville
  1455 Pleasant Hill Road, Lawrenceville, Georgia 30044
  P) 678-380-6730 F) 678-380-6715

- Guitar Center Marietta
  1901 Terrell Mill Rd. SE, Marietta, Georgia 30067
  P) 770-980-9222 F) 770-988-0267

- Jacksons Music
  5485 Westmoreland Plaza, Douglasville, GA 30135
  P) 770-949-5262
  www.jacksonsmusic.com

jacksonsmusic@earthlink.net

- Jacksons Music
  7445-A Old National Hwy., Riverdale, GA 30296
  P) 770-996-3680 F) 770-996-3789
  www.jacksonsmusic.com
  jacksonsmusic@hotlink.com

- Magic Audio
  Contact: Ben Cornthwaite
  204 14th St. NW, Atlanta, GA 30318
  P) 404-249-6336 F) 404-249-9422
  www.magicaudio.com

- Maple Street Guitars
  3199 Maple Drive, Atlanta, GA 30305
  P) 404-231-5214 F) 404-231-5529
  www.maplestreetguitars.com

- Music Go Round
  Beaver Ruin Village Shopping Center
  4153 Lawrenceville Hwy., Ste 8, Lilburn, GA 30047
  P) 770-931-9190 F) 770-931-7560
  www.musicgoround.com
  mgrlilburnga@charter.net

- Musiq World
  P) 770-621-2708
  www.muziq4u.com

- Pro Music Outlet
  4727 Memorial Dr., Decatur, GA 30032
  P) 404-294-5100
  www.promusicoutlet.com

- Sound Associates
  560-F Amsterdam Ave., Atlanta, GA 30306
  P) 404-724-9050 F) 404-724-9891
  www.soundassociates.com
  info@soundassociates.com

AUGUSTA MUSIC EQUIPMENT STORES

- Center Stage Music
  3830 Washington Rd., Suite 33, Martinez, GA 30907
  P) 706-860-8600 F) 706-868-0100
  www.centerstagemusic.com

- Jay's Music & Sound Super Center
  2702 Washington Rd., Augusta, GA 30309
  P) 706-736-1250

- Portman's Music
  2828 Milledgeville Rd., Augusta, GA 30904
  P) 706-738-1651
  www.portmansmusic.com

- Rock Bottom Music
  758 Broad Street, Augusta, GA 30901
  P) 706-724-1172 F) 706-724-0771
  www.rockbottommusic.com

MUSIC CONFERENCES

Music Conferences are a fantastic way to network, negotiate and know the business of music. By attending a music conference you have the ability to create windows of opportunity for yourself. This is achieved by first having a clearly identifiable goal. For instance, your goal may be to network with aspiring singers, songwriters and artist or to gather contact information from other industry decision-makers.

In addition, some music conferences have a T.V. and film component, which is a fantastic way to network with decision-makers who may be willing and able to get your music placed on T.V. and/or in a movie. As a music producer your goal should be to get your music heard in as many outlets as possible. Not only does this make you a more marketable music producer, but it also creates additional streams of revenue for you. Refer to page thirty-five for a list of music conferences.

MASTERING FACILITIES

Mastering is the art of fine-tuning an already fantastic song that has been properly mixed. Before you seek radio airplay, getting your song spun in clubs or mass-producing your music for retail sell, have your CD mastered by a mastering engineer. The mastering engineer should have years of experience and be familiar with mastering your style of music. Mastering a song is a technical science that normally requires years of experience by an educated professional.

Give yourself and your band a leg up over other artists and bands by having your music professionally mastered by a mastering engineer. Like other professionals on your team, you should interview the mastering engineer and ask for references of past and current clients. Below is a list of mastering engineers. Tell them you found them in the Atlanta Music Industry Connection Book by JaWar.

- Aucourant Records
  P.O. Box 2231, Roswell, GA 30077
  P) 770-640-9714
  www.aucourantrecords.com
  aucourant@aucourantrecords.com

- Atlanta Digital Mastering
  Premier Plaza, 194 Jonesboro Rd., Suite O-3
  Jonesboro, GA 30236
  P) 678-698-2301

- Digitak Mastering
  3603 MLK Blvd., Brunswick, GA 31520
  P) 912-264-8673

- Fulton Post Works
  3195 Buford Hwy., Suite 8, Duluth, GA 30096
  P) 770-476-4915

www.fultonpostworks.com
jfulton@fultonpostworks.com

- Glenn Schick Mastering
  3264 Shallowford Rd., Atlanta, GA 30341
  P) 770-451-1314 F) 770-457-5243
  www.gsmastering.com
  gsmastering@earthlink.net

- Griffin Mastering
  1051 Woodland Ave, Atlanta, GA 30316
  P) 404-622-5102
  www.mindspring.com/~gminc/
  gminc@mindspring.com

- HDQTRZ Digital Studios
  P) 404-643-8213
  www.hdqtrz.com
  earle@hdqtrz.com

- Nine Times Nine Entertainment
  P.O. Box 4727, Atlanta, Ga.30302
  P) 770-374-6306

- Pigpen Studios
  101 Surry Ct., Athens, GA 30606
  P) 706-369-6755
  www.pigpenstudios.net
  Daniel@pigpenstudios.net

- Sonare Recordings
  309 Gloucester Rd., Savannah, GA 31410
  P) 912-484-8451
  www.sonarerecordings.com

- Wave Guide Studios
  2062 Weems Road, Atlanta, GA 30084
  P) 770-939-2004 F) 770-938-4840
  www.waveguidestudios.com
  info@waveguidestudios.com

- Wizzard Media
  3500 Lenox Rd., Suite 1500, Atlanta, GA 30326

P) 404-321-3201 P) 800-352-8390 F) 404-633-0940
www.moneygrow.com/wizzard
wizard@moneygrow.com

Producer Websites Of Interest

Continuing your education and networking in the music industry will increase your opportunity for success. The sites below may prove to be beneficial to both music producer newcomers and seasoned professionals alike. Even if you are a platinum producer you will want to ensure that you maintain your success by building new bridges and staying ahead of the competition. The sites below will help you achieve those goals.

- www.atlantamusicproducers.com
- www.breakbeatvault.com
- www.dynamicproducer.com
- www.futureproducers.com
- www.iamusic.com
- www.justbeats.biz
- www.mpg.org.uk
- www.opuzz.com
- www.recordproduction.com
- www.royaltyfreemusic.com
- www.soundcrafting.com

How should a producer market their tracks?

1. Create & distribute a promotional instrumental CD; make sure your contact information is printed on all the CDs you hand out I.e. include phone numbers, e-mails, websites and your physical mailing address. I strongly suggest getting a low-priced voicemail number, free email account and post office box. You will want to get an economical voicemail number to ensure that you can pay the bill when times get tough. The worse thing is to have 1,000 plus CDs and flyers in the streets and all your contact information is wrong. The same rule

applies for the free e-mail account. In addition, by getting an email account you can correspond with people all over the world as long as you have access to the Internet. I like using a post office box, because the price is economical. In addition, the post office box affords you a certain amount of privacy and safety if you work from your home.

2. Create a website with streaming & downloadable tracks. This will allow you to market & promote your production services to the world 24/7 via the Internet.

3. Place your website address on every promotional item you hand out, including business cards.

4. Create mix CDs with the hottest artists rapping or singing over your tracks. Include some local talent on your mix CDs as well. This will ensure that you help grow the local music scene. In addition, the local artist will help promote the CD because they have a feature and vested interest in your success. If the Mix-CD is well received by the streets then the artist will benefit from the increased exposure. It is a win/win opportunity.

5. Submit your tracks to artists, managers, music publishers and attorneys that are seeking new music.

Producer's Revenue Stream

As a music producer you're in a unique position to earn an unlimited amount of money over time. The easiest way is to sell your tracks to the highest bidder. While selling your tracks to the highest bidder may turn you a quick profit, it may not be the most profitable way to earn your money. What is more profitable is to create opportunities where you generate multiple streams of revenue from the same track over time. This simply means you would earn money whenever your song is played.

Some of the ways your song may generate additional money is through music publishing, i.e. public performance, mechanical licenses, synchronization licenses and printed music, video games, downloadable ring tones, wireless devices, webscating, podcasting and digital performance royalties.

Mechanical royalties are paid from the sale of CDs and/or records. For example, as a producer you may get 3 points or 3% of the CD suggested retail price minus 10% or 15%. The ten or fifteen percent would go toward manufacturing & packaging the CD. Performance royalties are paid whenever a song you produced is played for the public. For instance, if the song is played on radio, t.v., cable, concert halls, and other music outlets you would be entitled to performance publishing royalties (money). These royalties are normally collected in the United States by three performance rights organizations or PROs. The PROs are ASCAP (American Society of Composers, Authors & Publishers), BMI (Broadcast Music Inc.) and SESAC (formerly known as the Society of European Stage Authors & Composers). Video games are also an excellent way to generate additional revenue. Many of the top game makers now have A&R (Artist & Repertoire) Departments.

Synchronization licenses are issued when your music is used in television, film or commercials i.e. jingles and infomercials. Depending on the popularity of the song, how your song is used and your clout as a music producer/composer, you may structure a deal where you receive a flat fee for how your song is to be played, a royalty each time the television program, film or commercial is aired or a combination of both. Structuring a deal that would pay a royalty each time your song is played would put you on the fast track to generating multiple steams of royalty revenue.

Printed music royalties are generated whenever your song is sold as sheet music. When the sheet music or lyrics of your song are displayed on a website, you are entitled to a royalty, especially if the website is generating income; an issue your entertainment attorney should address in depth with you.

Downloadable ring tones for cell phones and other wireless devices, is potentially a huge source of additional income. Whenever someone downloaded one of your tracks you should receive a royalty. Imagine receiving 10 cent per download; with millions of cell phone and wireless device users worldwide your earning potential is magnified. If you're interested in making your songs available as downloadable ring tones you may call me and I will put you in direct contact with one of my industry sources. There is a small fee for this contact, but with magnified earnings potential it will be worth every nickel. For details contact me toll-free at 800-963-0949 or jawar@mt101.com

Webcasting & digital performance royalties are relatively new, but the money making potential for music producers is enormous. To ensure you receive your webcasting & digital performance royalties you will need to send Soundexchange a Producers Letter of Direction. As a the copyright owner of your music you may be entitled to additional webcasting royalties under the Copyright Act. Remember that selling your tracks for a flat fee is only one way to generate money from your music. As a music producer you could create multiple income streams through music publishing, video games, downloadable ring tones, wireless devices, webcasting, podcasting and digital performance royalties.

- Publishing royalties

    1. Mechanical Licenses-CD & Record Sales
    2. Synchronization Licenses-Television, film, commercials i.e. jingles & infomercials
    3. Public Performance-radio airplay
    4. Printed Music-lyric or sheet music

- Touring-concert ticket sales
- Merchandising-t-shirts, hats, shoes, belts, etc. sold at retail stores, concerts, on the Internet, through direct mail and catalog sales
- Guest appearances on other artists songs
- Product and/or service endorsements
- Video Games
- Downloadable Ringtones & other wireless devices
- Webcasting & Digital Performance Royalties
- Producers should read the Creating Wealth Section on page 147 to increase their investing knowledge

PRODUCERS BOOKS

Atlanta Music Industry Connection: Resources for Producers by JaWar

MANAGER'S CORNER

What skills do I need to succeed as a manager?

As an artist manager a few of the many skills you should possess include the ability to seek and develop star talent, be extremely organized, professional, know the business of music, have extensive contacts in the industry and genre of which you seek to develop star talent and above all, be honest and truly believe in the artist you are managing.

As a manager you may have to be a husband, wife, mother, father, brother, sister and friend to the artist you are managing. Meaning at various times in the artists career you may have to play the role of any one of these persons to comfort and support your artist.

In addition, the manager should have some knowledge of contract negotiations, how record companies operate, basic bookkeeping and/or accounting skills and be computer and Internet literate.

What are the three types of managers?

1. **Artist Manager**-An artist manager may be responsible for finding and developing star talent and navigating an artist's career to create and maximize "fame equity."

2. **Business Manager**-A business manager normally handles the financial affairs of the artist to ensure that the artist spends less money than they make. In addition, the business manager may help to diversify the artist's financial assets i.e. investing in real estate, the stock market, bonds and other businesses, to ensure that the artist is able to maintain a certain standard of living and invest money for retirement.

NOTE: The artist should always write their own checks or have a system that allows the artists to closely monitor the business manager's activity. Trust is fantastic; accountability is better.

3. **Road Manager**-A road manager is responsible for a number of tasks while the artist is touring. For example, the road manager will ensure that all the contractual arrangements made with the venue have been met. In addition, the road manager will ensure that the artist arrives promptly for all the promotional appearances, such as in-stores, radio, print media and other engagements to promote the tour.

Who pays the manager?

The artist normally pays the manager. Remember the artist manager works for the artist.

How much money are artist managers paid?

Artist managers typically get between 5% to 25% of an artist's gross earnings. However, if you are an artist you will want to negotiate paying your manager from your net earnings vs. your gross earnings. Gross earnings means before taxes, while net earnings mean after your taxes have been paid. So, if the manager gets paid from the gross earnings they will receive a larger portion of the artist royalties (money).

When do I need an entertainment attorney?

A manager should seek a qualified entertainment attorney before signing any contracts. In some instances a manager may also seek the services of an attorney to negotiate contracts on their behalf.

May the manager also be the artist's attorney?

Yes, although in some instances it may be a conflict of interest. For example, since there should be a written contract between the artist and manager, the attorney who is also the artist manager may not draft (write) and execute (make happen) the best contract for the artist between the artist and manager, since the attorney is also the manager.

How do I find new talent?

First, you may find new talent by going to open-mics, talent showcases and music conferences. Second, you may place a classified ad and/or distribute flyers at music retail stores, schools and music industry networking events letting people know that you are seeking to manage new talent. Finally, you may use music groups on-line to locate new talent. For instance, www.yahoo.com, www.msn.com and www.google.com all have music groups where you can become a member and post information about the business of music for networking sake. Craigslist.com is also a free website that allows you to post information to certain groups. I have received a number of responses by using www.craigslist.com.

MANAGEMENT COMPANIES

Often, I meet artist who say "do you know any managers?" my reply is "Yes! They are in my book the Atlanta Music Industry Connection." The artist normally replies with something like, "Yeah, yeah, yeah, but do you know any managers *personally*?" and I reply "Yes! They are in my book the Atlanta Music Industry Connection." Many times the artist has this frustrated look on their face that says does JaWar not understand all I want are one or two manager names and phone numbers and not some book on the music industry?

At this point I will ask the artist a few questions like, "What can a manager do for you that you can not do for yourself? What do you expect from your manager? Who will pay the manager? How much money will the manager get paid? Why should a manager take you as a client? What makes you special from all the other artist in the market place? How many unreleased hit records do you have? Do you have a website? Do you have an e-mail list of fans? How often do you perform? What is your monthly marketing budget? (Be it $50 or $5,000 a month.) Do you have a typed bio and professional photos of yourself? Has your music been professionally recorded, mixed and mastered? What are your career goals? What are your professional goals? Do you have any mental problems (smile)? What if anything is preventing you from dedicating all of your time to your music craft? Do you have a job or some source of monthly income? Finally, why do you create, record and perform music?"

This line of questioning allows me and more importantly the artist, to determine how well they have thought through their own planning process. In addition, the goal is to get the artist to see that there is plenty of work that they can do themselves before seeking a manager, by doing so several things tend to happen. First, the artists begin to empower themselves. Second, the artist gains a greater appreciation for the manager's job. Third, the artist will better know what type of manager they need to help them accomplish their goals and realize their potential. Finally, the artist will see that with a bit of planning their career could be on the fast track to success.

Most managers will appreciate this line of questioning, as it will help them determine how serious an artist is to perfecting their craft and achieving their goals. When contacting the managers below let them know you found them in the Atlanta Music Industry Connection Book by JaWar.

- 228 Management & Consulting, LLC
  194 Holtzclaw St., Atlanta, GA 30316
  P) 404-931-3391 F) 404-350-3405
  nbrison@comcast.net

- Alliance Artist
  1225 N. Meadow Pkwy, Suite 100, Roswell, GA 30076
  P) 770-663-4240 F) 770-663-8757

- Artist Control Management
  685 Lambert Dr., NE, Atlanta, GA 30324
  P) 404-733-5511 F) 404-733-5512

- Artist Management International
  P.O. Box 671837, Atlanta, GA 30006
  P) 770-428-5484 F) 770-514-9710

- Bossman Entertainment
  P.O. Box 56732, Atlanta, GA 30343
  P) 404-402-3607
  2bossworld@yahoo.com

- Brash Management
  Contact: Richard Dunn
  658 11th St., Atlanta, GA 30318
  P) 678-904-4790
  www.brashmusic.com
  dunn@brashmusic.com

- Brown Cat, Inc.

400 Foundry St., Athens, GA 30601
P) 706-354-8301 F) 770-369-1631

- Dailey's Entertainment
  Contact: Moses Daily
  P.O. Box 13365, Atlanta, GA 30324
  P) 404-239-8062 F) 404-241-8869
  mosesdaily@aol.com

- Daycare Management & Consulting
  Contact: Brad McDonald
  450 Ashburton Ave., Atlanta, GA 30317
  P) 404-243-0213 F) 404-243-0813 Cell) 404-277-9838
  www.daycaremgmt.com
  daycaremgmt@mindspring.com

- Elevation Management
  Contact: E. Anthony Daniel
  5300 Memorial Dr, # 201-E Stone Mountain, GA 30083
  P) 404-508-9017
  eadaniel@bellsouth.net

- Ghost Riders Entertainment
  280 Northern Ave 30-J, Avondale Estates, GA 30002
  P) 404-587-2300
  www.ghostridersentetainment.com
  ghost@ghostridersentertainment.com

- Goldston & Associates Entertainment Management
  Contact: Nathaniel Russell Goldston IV "Russ"
  82 Piedmont Ave., Atlanta, GA 30303
  P) 404-550-6164
  nbreden@yahoo.com

- Iron Man Management
  305 Willow Ridge Way, Avondale Estates, GA 30002
  P) 404-914-4900
  Sean_brite@yahoo.com

- J-Pat Management
  Contact: Jonetta Patton
  3996 Pleasantdale Rd., #104-A, Doraville, GA 30340
  P) 770-416-8619 F) 770-409-2385

- Jess Rosen
  3423 Piedmont Rd., #200, Atlanta, GA 30305
  P) 404-237-7700 F) 404-237-5260

- Marvelous Enterprises
  2020 Howell Mill Rd., Suite C-109, Atlanta, GA 30318
  P) 404-367-9122 F) 404-367-9123

- Midnight Management
  Contact: David Freeman
  4247 Orchard Grove, Stone Mountain, GA 30083
  P) 404-508-9690
  Fortknox76@yahoo.com

- Music Business Associates
  Contact: Dominique Mitchell
  P.O. Box 830513, Stone Mountain, GA 30083
  P) 678-656-9823
  www.officialmba.com
  contact@officialmba.com

- Music Management Incorporated
  541 10th Street, Suite 230, Atlanta, GA 30318
  P) 866-664-0808 F) 770-673-0808
  musicmgtinc@aol.com

- Nu South Productions
  P.O. Box 566954, Atlanta, GA 31156
  P) 678-508-1489
  Djquest_nusouth@yahoo.com

- Own Music
  Contact: Dayo Adebiyi or Al Thrash
  2451 Cumberland Pkwy, Ste 3516, Atlanta, GA 30339
  P) 770-413-7440
  www.ownmusic.com
  dayo.adebiyi@ownmusic.com

- Priceless Music Management
  2771 Lawrenceville Hwy #206, Atlanta, GA 30033
  P) 770-724-1933 F) 770-724-1987

- Red Carpet Music
  P.O. Box 501581, Atlanta, GA 31150
  P) 770-396-0881 F) 770-396-0842
  www.redcarpetmusic.com
  info@redcarpetmusic.com

- SSP Management
  816 Covered Bridge Way, Fairburn, GA 30213
  P) 404-886-3578
  www.soularsausage.com
  sspmanagement@gmail.com

- The Woodland Entertainment Group, Inc.
  Contact: Kirk D. Woods
  2870 Peachtree Rd., Suite 226, Atlanta, GA 30305
  P) 404-378-0334 F) 404-378-8120
  woodlandent@hotmail.com

- Tri-State Empire Management
  4247 Orchard Grove, Stone Mountain, GA 30083
  P) 404-508-9690 F) 678-325-2030
  www.williejoe.com
  tristateempire@gmail.com

- Woods Entertainment
  244 Underwood Dr., Atlanta, GA 30328
  P) 404-433-4585
  www.woodsentertainment.net
  tim@woodsentertainment.net

MANAGEMENT BOOKS

- All Area Access:
  Personal Management for Unsigned Musicians
  By Marc Davison

- Atlanta Music Industry Connection: Resources for
  Managers
  By JaWar

- Booking & Tour Management for the Performing Arts
  By Rena Shagan

- Business of Artist Management
  By Xavier M. Frascogna Jr. & H. Lee Hetherington

- Choosing a Manager
  By John E. Kali

- Managing Artists in Pop Music
  By Mitch Weiss and Perri Gaffney

- Managing Your Band
  By Dr. Stephen Marcone

- The Game of Hip Hop Artist Management
  By Walt Goodridge
  www.hiphopbiz.com

- The IMF Handbook:
  A Guide to Professional Band Management

MANAGEMENT ORGANIZATIONS

- Indie Managers Association
  www.indiemanagers.com
  indie@indiemanagers.com

- International Music Managers Forum
  www.immf.net

- Music Managers Forum
  www.mmfus.com

- National Conference of Personal Managers
  www.ncopm.com
  askncopm@ncopm.com

Interview with Dayo & Al of Own Music

JaWar: What's your name?

Dayo: Dayo Adebiyi

Al: I'm Al Thrash

JaWar: How long have each of you been in the music industry?

Dayo: Since '95

JaWar: How about you Al?

Al: About 10 years

JaWar: How did you get started in the music business?

Dayo: I go back to junior high, high school, rapping with classmates and hanging out. I'm from the west coast, so I came up right around the time where for whatever reason the west coast was hot and there were a lot of acts out there, so you were more than likely to have friends who ran in different circles with artist who were getting deals and what not. Hieroglyphics was one of those camps that I ran with back then. I focused on my school and my interest in music because of my social circle. I wanted to see what kind of went on behind the scenes and was really interested [in the business of music]. So that's kind of what got me into it. In terms of working, once I got out here and went to Morehouse in 92', I had some other friends from California who were here working in the industry doing street teamwork, consulting and promotions. Hanging around them and just learning the lifestyle that you could achieve and reach. Not so much about the money but setting your own schedule and the   freedom.

JaWar:How about you Al?

Al: With me it started coming out of high school,
        freshman year of college, I had some friends that
        ran parties. Back in '92, '93 it was nothing like you
        see in Atlanta now, with the whole party thing.
        There were one or two guys, who'd do a party
        Christmas Night, Thanksgiving Night and maybe
        two parties over the summer. These guys were
        friends of my sister. They knew I was a freshman in
        the AUC (Atlanta University Center) and I could
        attract a lot of people for them in terms of freshmen
        and sophomores, so I just started doing parties and
        that more or less got me acclimated to promotions.
        When people see you around passing some flyers
        then a lot of people come to you and they come to
        your party. I knew that record labels gave out music
        and they love to know that we could get a crowd
        together for their artist. So I started calling [record
        companies] and getting CDs and posters to give
        out. So that's how it started. Arista was the first
        company I called and they were really taking care
        of us back then.

**JaWar:Both of you mentioned that you've been to college.
        Is that where you met?**

Al: Mmmmmm yeah, yeah!

Dayo: We both went to Morehouse and I'd see Al around
        campus. I was an intern at BMG and he started
        working with Arista and that's when we linked up.

Al: It was one of those things where I knew Dayo did
        something with music on campus. I would come
        into a marketing class while he was leaving. You
        always had that 10 or 15 minutes of talk time, 'have

you heard this new CD da da da...' and we just kept that going and that's what brought us together.

JaWar: Do you think that college has prepared you for the music industry in terms of artist management?

Al: I definitely think it has. I think that college has prepared me for a lot, everything that I do in life "really" but specifically music. One thing about college is it took a whole city and shrunk it into a campus. So to me, the AU (Atlanta University) Center where there were three or four schools there to me that was a replica of Atlanta, even more so a replica of the US, because you got people coming from all over. And so on that campus you have artists, producers, business people, rich kids, poor kids, etc. So just in learning how to deal with people with different lifestyles and backgrounds, embrace creativity, see all the different kinds of things from opposite sides of the country or whatever; I do feel that it prepared me for working in the industry.

Dayo: I have a little different take on that. I think school prepared me for what's necessary in terms of trying to be upwardly mobile within the entertainment industry, in terms of networking skills and things like that. I think in a campus environment there are not nearly as many individuals who are going to be out to do whatever they have to do to get to their objective. Whereas in the [music] industry you'll find it's so cut throat and scrupulous it doesn't matter they'll [people in the music industry] run right through you if they have the opportunity. They don't try to create their own business, so in that regard, college and framework didn't necessarily prepare me for that experience but our work experience as well. School enabled us to at least get a taste of what was to come and some of the transition.

JaWar:If you could sum it up in a sentence or two, how would you define artist management?

Al: I would define it as the necessary business that's needed to bring creativity to the marketplace. Meaning managing an artist or producer, everything from label or business relations for this artist or producer, dealing with whatever entity is releasing the music managing or taking care of the process of doing work and of work ethics. Everything from how well their music is recorded to the types of outlets that you try to get it out in just managing that entire process and making sure that the artist is aware of all of the steps in the value chain so that as your creating the music that goes ten different places, they are aware that this person, this entity has to do this to it so we have to make sure, before it gets out the door, we know business wise, publishers, where it's going, sales wise, dealing with the label, where its going and what needs to be done with that music to get it there.

JaWar:What skills does a person need to become an artist manager or to succeed as an artist manager?

Dayo: I think you need a lot of interpersonal skills. It's a relationship business. You go furthest based upon the way you hold your head above rising waters. I also feel that managing an artist is basically a lot of faith, hoping that you're going to be guiding them right, steering them and also have a vision of your own that should coincide with your client to get that person or group where they want to be. [As a manager] you're a service provider. You want to provide the best service. It helps get you to your objectives without loosing who you are as well.

Al: A lot of it is empowering the artist or our client with many of the things that we're doing. Many times you look at an artist manager relationship and the artist is just doing music, they are clueless to what happens once they hand that CD or mix tape over. I find that when an artist is empowered about the industry and about the marketplace then that makes for a better working relationship and things tend to thrive little bit better.

JaWar: Could you give three or four responsibilities of an artist manager?

Dayo: Representation, business management, empowerment and education.

JaWar: How about you Al, would you say that about the same?

Al: Yeah, I would definitely say the same and another major responsibility about artist management is getting the money.

JaWar: Explain that a little bit.

Al: When the artist makes the decision that they are going to make music professionally and this is how they're going to eat and live, it's different types of avenues out there to exploit a copyright just to make the most money and get a possible offer off of the copyright, meaning a song or whatever. It doesn't just come to you, you put an album out, that's great, its up to us to seek out soundtrack opportunities, commercials, just get to places where we can make the most money possible for our artist and in turn for ourselves. It doesn't happen from us just going about our day to day [business], we have to be very proactive about it.

JaWar: Could you give one example of how you were able to do that for one of your previous or current clients i.e. one specific example of how you were able to take a song they did and actually use it beyond the CD that they released?

Al: Yeah! For example, Killer Mike's, "Action Song" was the lead single for his album. The song itself was not hugely accepted radio wise, but the format of the song, the tempo and feel made it very appealing to the video game culture. It has that kind of feel and it's on Madden 4 the EA Sports Game as the lead song. In some ways you have to play the cards you're dealing with; hopefully if you can keep your hand alive then something is going to happen.

JaWar: I'm going to go back to that because our readers want to know the specifics without getting into the menial aspects. How were you able to get Killer Mike's song onto that video game? I mean did you call the person [at EA Sports], did they seek you out, and how did it work? What were the specific steps you took on getting the song used?

Dayo: Al and I really started trying to heighten the awareness and profile of the artist himself and subsequently his music. It started prior to the release of his album. EA Sports and most of the video game companies now have separate music departments and even A&R's that are assigned specifically to oversee the talent and music that they put on these games. And this particular A&R was amongst a circle so we linked up and reached out and saw that sometime earlier he was already aware of Killer Mike and once the album came out he was able to hear all the music he felt that that song fit his game Madden 4. Mike had done the previous Madden, Madden 3 and had success with that. [The Madden Game] ships about 4 million copies out the gate [so your not] going to deny it but he reached out to us, because he'd been aware of Killer Mike.

83

AI: In reaching out to us he identified a song amongst a few songs that we presented and that song seemed to work, but we just needed to make some changes, obviously to really fit that format. Mike already had a lot of football references in the song but in speaking with the A&R he let us know what kind of things Mike really needed to draw upon. We got back with Mike and said well this is a great opportunity they want accept it the way it is now, but we could go back and do X, Y & Z, it could be a big hit on the video game scene. We went back to the lab he made a few changes on it lyric wise and we sent it out and it was exactly what they were looking for.

JaWar: Was there a lot of red tape in terms of possible clearances with Aquemini Records, given that is the label that he was or is signed to right now?

Dayo: At that point, there wasn't so much from what I can remember and I think a lot of that really is due to when this kind of went down; right after the album came out, probably a month or so after the album came out. Unfortunately sales wise that album didn't meet any of our expectations. You know it sold, but for the sweat we put into it, two years working on it, of course we wanted it to sell in a day what it sold in those two or three months. Just for that reason here's an opportunity to keep that artist out there [in the public light] and legally it is PA and so, you know, we're going to get paid for it. So, it wasn't so much red tape as I hear some other situations may come up and the label is like 'no', you know...

JaWar: How did you meet Killer Mike?

AI: I actually went to High School with Killer Mike.

JaWar: What High School was that?

84

Al: Frederick Douglass High School here in Atlanta. Yeah, so we actually graduated together. I had known him since around 8th or 9th grade. We stayed in contact. Mike went to Morehouse as well, so we stayed in contact there, I knew he was doing music and I started doing music as well. Over the years I ended up moving to Nashville doing some work out there. We lost contact for a year or two then we caught back up. I knew he was doing music. Really his sheer talent allowed him to pop up on the Outkast album. He just rapped for Big Boi one day and they were like 'I got to have you'. I definitely give him props for that because his sheer talent got him to where he is now. We just stayed in contact he kept it going and he got into the deal situation where we had an opportunity for us to work with him and really get him developed.

JaWar: How do you feel that you were able to help develop Killer Mike's career? Taking him from just rapping on the corner, if you will, to rapping for Outkast, to maybe helping him get signed, closing the deal and doing EA sports?

Dayo: I think our biggest benefit was probably giving him some understanding as to what the industry is all about. Not necessarily the parties and long nights at the studio, but the true work that goes into it from the grass roots approach. He had been surrounded by half these guys who were all multi-platinum plus artists! It had been a long time since they had a real developing artist go through the steps of development, so I think exposing him and letting him understand what is necessary to break as a new artist in the market is invaluable as well as giving him a perspective in his own right. How he viewed things and what he personally chose to make his path so he's not a carbon copy of someone else. He tried to create his own identity, which we value more than anything else.

Al: We had a lot of relationships from our past dealings in the industry at BMG, with DJ's, retailers and record storeowners across the country. So once the album came through the pipeline we had people along those lines in various markets. I lived in Nashville for three years and Nashville was the number two-radio market for a single, the relationships that we had with radio in Nashville got a lot of sales for Mike's release.

JaWar:How does a manager get paid, how do you get paid?

Dayo: What we've done is we've set up a company, that's how we look at our artists or our producers, we set these companies up and we get percentages of that. Generally that's 15%-20%. We really try to look at the people who deal with us as almost media companies in their own right. Everyone's trying to get their word, their voice out and it speaks kind of wide. They're media companies just like TNT or CBS.

JaWar:That 15%-20% is that Gross or Net of what those companies bring in?

Dayo: That's gross.

Al: And ideally in terms of at what point the artist is in his career, if we are actually developing this artist for the sake of getting a record deal and go and land a deal then that percentage of the deal as well. It tends to still be about 15%- 20% when we go and land a deal. That's obviously if, you're talking about a huge budget, that's a big payoff. Along the way, that is if you did shows, if they license a song, if they asked for an appearance etc. that's 15% - 20% of that. It's in our interest to be pro-active, make as many calls as we can make, get as much work done because artists really when we would ideally want our artist working 350 days out the year.

JaWar:What's the name of your company?

Dayo: Own Music

JaWar:If people wanted to get in contact with you, how would they do that?

Dayo: They can email al.thrash@ownmusic.com as well as dayo.adebiyi@ownmusic.com or they can call us at 770-413-7440.

JaWar:Any closing comments?

Al: One thing I would say is right now Own Music is managing a 14 year old name Shorthand his 21-year-old brother is his producer, One Will productions. We've been working with them for about 2 years now, they just moved to Atlanta, so we're very excited about that. We're looking to fill that void of that younger artist right now, whether he's not really out there, but we're doing some big boy stuff, that's what the music is going to be focused on in 2004. We are looking at continuing to expand our line up.

Dayo: I'd just like to note one reason why I started the company, it's like, we were going to venture away from BMG, which was a comfortable check at the time because we really believed in the artists. We try to make certain that we keep the integrity with all of our clients and the integrity of the music and it's something that they create and they own that's why we created the name Own Music. When people in the shower singing or in the basement cooking up beats, walking the walk humming, we want them out and we will market them, promote that in a way that would benefit them. Not just anything, like the large distributors, Sony, BMG, WEA, or whatever. In a lot of ways music is like that, for a young kid specifically to get out given current situations and we want to make certain that they have the opportunity to do that.

JaWar: Appreciate it

MANAGER'S REVENUE STREAM

Remember that managers receive anywhere from 5%-20% of the artist's gross or net income. Refer to the Artist Development Chapter to see the various ways artists are paid.

If I were a manager, I would seek to get paid from the artist gross income. If I were the artist, I would seek to pay the manager from my net income. At the end of the day the business arrangement must be a win/win for both parties. Know what you want, negotiate your terms and be willing to give a lot to get a lot! Managers should read the Creating Wealth Section on page 147 and encourage the artist(s) and producer(s) they represent to do the same to increase their knowledge on investing.

INFORMATION FOR ALL

Six ways to protect yourself in the industry

1. Own and control your copyrights
2. Own and control your music publishing
3. Own and control the rights, name, and likeness to your stage name and image (trademark & servicemark your stage name) Own and control your domain name i.e. www.yourstagename.com
4. Always have a competent music entertainment attorney review and draft your contracts.
5. Attempt not to sign long-term exclusive contracts; if you do, you better do number four.
6. Have multiple streams of revenue (making money)

What Copyright Forms do I need?

You will need copyright Form PA & Form SR. PA stands for performing arts while SR stands for sound recording.

Obtain copyright forms through:

- Library of Congress, Copyright Office,
  Register of Copyrights, 101 Independence Avenue, S.E.,
  Washington, D.C. 20559-6000
  P) 202-707-3000
  lcweb.loc.gov

  Copyright Order Form Hotline
  P) 202-707-9100

What is the price to register a copyright?

When this book was printed the price to register a copyright through the U.S. Library of Congress was $30. You may copyright a collection of songs under one title for $30 as long as the author of all the songs is the same.

Gordon Publishing sales a copyright kit.

- P) 678-698-7776

How do I protect my band name & logo in GA?

Apply for a trademark with the Georgia Secretary of State.

How do I contact the GA Secretary of State?

- Office of Secretary of State Corporation Division, Suite 315, West Tower, 2 MLK Dr., Atlanta, GA 30334
  P) 404-656-2861 F) 404-657-6380
  www.sos.state.ga.us

How do I protect my band name and logo in the United States?

To protect an artist stage name, a band's name and/or logo apply for a trademark or servicemark through the U.S. Patent & Trademark Office.

- U.S. Patent and Trademark Office
  General Information Services Division
  Crystal Plaza 3, RM 2 C02
  Washington, D.C. 20231
  P) 800-786-9199
  www.uspto.gov

When do I need a business license or tax I.D.?

When one wants to establish the business entity separate from the business owner they should apply for a business license and tax I.D. For instance, your personal checking account should be different from your business checking account.

What is the difference between a business license and a tax I.D.?

A business license grants you the right to legally do business in a city or county. A Federal Employer Identification Number (Tax I.D.) is used to identify your business entity with the I.R.S (Internal Revenue Service). You will want to obtain your business license and Tax I.D. before opening your business checking account.

How do I get a business license?

Normally, a business license may be obtained by contacting the local or county tax office. In most instances this information may be found either on the Internet, in the Local Yellow Pages or by contacting 411.

What is a tax I.D.?

An EIN (Employer Identification Number) sometimes called a Federal Identification Number (F.I.N) is used to identify business entities. If you are starting a Partnership, LLC (Limited Liability Company) or corporation you will need to apply for an EIN through the I.R.S. at www.irs.gov. Having a Tax I.D. is paramount (vital) for obtaining business credit.

How do I get a tax I.D.?

To obtain a tax I.D. (EIN/FIN) contact the I.R.S. at www.irg.gov. EIN's are free through the I.R.S.

What is Dun & Bradstreet?

Dun & Bradstreet is a credit rating agency for businesses. In addition, Dun & Bradstreet tracks the credit worthiness of businesses much like Equifax, Experian and Transunion tracks the credit worthiness of individuals.

How may I contact Dun & Bradstreet?

- D&B Corp., 103 JFK Pkwy, Short Hills, NJ 07078
  P) 800-234-3867
  custserv@dnb.com

Where may I get business cards for free?

- www.vistaprint.com or www.buyprintingdirect.com

How may I get flyers printed for free?

First, determine who may need to promote their business in the city. Remember the business does not necessarily have to be music related. For instance, a local clothing store, real estate agent or car dealership, may want to promote their business. Second, the business should be one that has the money, but not the time to distribute the flyers. Third, set up a meeting with the possible candidates. Fourth, let them know that you are an aspiring artist, producer, manager or engineer seeking a co-op (cooperative) opportunity to help spread the word about your businesses. Propose that they get one side of the flyer to promote their business and that you get the other to promote yours. Next propose that they pay for the printing of the flyers and that you distribute them. Inform them that because your business is promoted on one-side of the flyer that you have a "VESTED INTEREST" in insuring that the flyers are properly distributed. Remember to use the words "VESTED INTEREST" it has a very professional tone to it. Before you approach any one, remember that your typed proposal has the following details the printing company you will be using, the exact price for printing, shipping and taxes if applicable, turnaround time (time it will take to get the flyers back) and your distribution points (drop-off locations).

How may I get 50 to 100 Promo CDs FREE?

You may either check the Local Sunday Newspaper or visit the websites of the following stores Best Buy, Circuit City, Staples, Office Max, and Office Depot for their rebate specials. Normally, **one of the stores will have a special offer where you may purchase anywhere from 50 to 100 CD-Rs for free via their rebate program.** Remember to keep your original receipt, barcode from the packaging and get the necessary rebate forms from the store.

All of the rebate specials are subject to certain terms, so ensure that you read all the fine print. For example, most of the programs are designed where you are only eligible (able) to get one rebate offer per person per household. In addition, there usually are expiration dates for the rebate programs.

Sometimes the rebate offers for CD-Rs may not be for free, but for a substantial discount. For instance, you may be able to purchase 50 CD-Rs for only $4.99 through the rebate program.

Once you have your blank CDs you simply need to burn (record) your music on them. Now you have anywhere from 50 to 100 promotional CDs. These may be used in your press kits, given away as promotional material or sold to fans.

Where may I use the Internet for free?

Most public libraries, the Department of Labor and Goodwill locations provide free Internet access. Some even offer access to Microsoft Word, Excel and PowerPoint for typing letters, invoices, proposals and presentations, etc. You will find that each library has its on way of doing things, so check around, find the one that works best for you and start using the Internet for free.

How may I get a free e-mail account?

You may get a free e-mail account at www.yahoo.com, www.hotmail.com, www.google.com, www.juno.com, www.lycos.com and www.fastmail.com. There are other free e-mail account systems, but these may be the most popular on the Internet.

If you are serious about creating windows of opportunities for yourself in the music business, you will need to have access to the Internet and an e-mail account. It is not up for debate.

What is a One-Sheet?

A one-sheet is an industry standard document used to inform retailers, one-stops and distributors about a new release. One-sheets are used for both CD and Book releases. A one-sheet contains the following:

- CD/Book Cover Artwork
- Barcode Number
- Suggested Retail Price
- Wholesale Price
- Record/Distributor Contact Details for Ordering product
- Special Artist Mention i.e. is there any platinum artists, writers or producers featured on the project, etc.

What is a Split Sheet?

A split sheet is a document that shows who the writer(s), producer(s) and musician(s) are of a particular song. More importantly it easily identifies what percentage each person contributed to a song. A split sheet is a simple way to keep everyone involved in creating a song honest. Songwriters and producers should not leave a recording session without having completed a split sheet.

Every recording studio, songwriter, producer, musician, manager, entertainment attorney and music business professional should have a few copies on hand. Split sheets are included in the How To Press 1,000 Retail Ready CD's Without Using Your On Money Kit. Details about the kit may be found at the end of the book.

What is Soundexchange?

Soundexchange is responsible for collecting and distributing performance royalties in the digital media arena i.e. digital distribution, from such entities as webcasters, satellite radio and Internet radio service providers to producers, recording artists and copyright owners. If you are a music producer, recording artist or copyright owner and your music is being broadcast through a digital media, (For example, satellite radio, internet radio and/or cable/direct tv radio) you may be loosing money by not registering your song with Soundexchange. You may be a member of either ASCAP, BMI or SESAC and collect royalties from Soundexchange as well.

How do I contact Soundexchange?

- Soundexchange
  1330 Connecticut Ave. NW
  Suite 330 Washington, DC 20036
  P) 202-828-0120 F) 202-833-2141
  www.soundexchange.com

Where do music professionals network?

That really depends on the genre of music. However, you can normally find music professionals at Music Conferences like Music Therapy 101, Music Festivals like the Sweet Auburn Festival, Smith's Old Bar, concerts sponsored by radio stations and strip clubs!

You should always have promotional material with you, as you never know when you are going to meet someone in the music business that could change your life. Always have promotional flyers, CDs and business cards at your disposal.

MUSIC RETAIL STORES

Getting your music sold in retail stores is simple if you have done your homework. Before approaching music stores you should have built a loyal following. This is achieved by performing regularly, distributing flyers, getting CD reviews and interviews in local and regional music publications, having a website where fans can visit to get updates on you and sending regular emails to new and existing fans.

While building a loyal fan base, an artist will want to build solid relationships with music retailers. For example, visit local music stores at least once a month and ask the manager or owner what music is selling the most. Ask what those artists are doing to create such a demand for their product. Ask the manager or owner for suggestions for creating a buzz for a new artist. If you listen you will learn far more than you would imagine.

After doing these things you will know when it is time to put your new release in music retail stores.

What is consignment?

Consignment is where you leave your product (CDs, t-shirts, books, etc.) with the retailer to sell for a pre-determined price. For instance, you may sell your CD to the store for $8.00 and the store may resell your CD for $13.99. Once your CD is actually sold to a customer, then you are due your $8.00 from the store. You are paid your money only after your product is sold. While it is always advantageous to get your money up front from retailers, most stores will choose to put your music on consignment. After your CD has demonstrated a degree of success some stores will opt to buy your CDs outright from you. Consignment works the same for CDs, t-shirts, artwork and books.

To ensure that you don't miss any retail sales, I recommend you create two call days a month. Your call day will be a specific time and day that you will contact retail stores to get inventory details. For instance, you may call stores on the first and third Monday of every month between 10:00am and 12:00pm. During these call time you will simply ask the retailer how many CDs or books, etc. are currently in stock. For instance, during my call days I will contact the stores and say "Good Morning, I'm JaWar. Will you tell me how many copies of the Atlanta Music Industry Connection Books you have left?"

Call days help you achieve several things. First, they help you maintain a working relationship with retailers. Second, it demonstrates to the retailer that you are serious about your project and have a system for monitoring sales. Thirdly, by having call days you will know when it is time to visit the store to either sell them more CDs, books, etc. and/or collect your money from product left on consignment. This will help you control your inventory so that you know how much product to order and when. This will help you maintain better cash flow. In addition, over time you know which stores are your bulls and which ones are your bears. Bulls being the stores that sell the highest volume of your product and bears being the stores that sell the lowest volume of your product in a relative time period (i.e. over 30, 60 or 90 days). Keep in mind that every sale is a product sold and at the end of the day it all adds up. Below are stores you should begin contacting. Tell them that JaWar, author of the Atlanta Music Industry Connection Book referred you.

- Alegria Musical - Spanish Speaking
  6289 S. Norcross-Tucker Rd., Suite-C
  Tucker, GA 30084
  P) 678-822-6006 P) 678-468-6836

- Backstage Music
  7195-C Highway 85, Riverdale, GA 30274
  P) 770-996-5566

- Bernard's Records
  3579 M.L. King Jr., Atlanta, GA 30031
  P) 404-699-0669

- Big Oomp Records
  Attn: Store Promotions Dept.
  1079 MLK Drive NW, Ste 2, Atlanta, GA 30314

- Big Oomp Records
  1120 Ralph D. Abernathy, Suite 2, Atlanta, GA 30314
  P) 404-758-4210

- Big Oomp Records
  751 Simpson Rd., NW, Atlanta, GA 30314

- Big Oomp Records
  1954 Candler Rd., Decatur, GA 30032

- Big Oomp Records
  2925 Headland Dr., East Point, GA 30311
  P) 404-344-4711

- Big Oomp Records
  2668 Campbellton Rd., SW, Atlanta, GA 30311
  P) 404-349-0620

- Big Oomp Records
  813 Concord Rd., Smyrna, GA 30080
  P) 770-436-7767

- Casablanca Musica Y Libros – Spanish Speaking
  1250 Tech Dr., Suite 445, Norcross, GA 30093
  P) 770-925-7300 F) 770-925-7342

- Circle Sky Records
  3633-E Chamblee-Tucker Rd
  Embry Village Shopping Center, Atlanta, GA 30341
  P) 770-491-2100
  www.circleskyrecords.com
  info@circleskyrecords.com

- Corner Compact Disc, Inc.
  1048 N. Highland Ave., NE, Atlanta, Georgia 30306
  P) 404-875-3087 F) 404-875-3088
  www.cornercd.com
  cornercd@mindspring.com

- Criminal Records
  466 Moreland Ave. Atlanta, GA 30307-1925
  P) 404-215-9511 F) 404-659-0320
  www.criminal.com

- DBS Sounds
  5658 Riverdale Rd., Ste-P, College Park, GA 30349
  P) 770-997-5776
  www.dbssounds.com

- DBS Sounds
  4841 Jonesboro Rd., Forest Park, GA 30297
  P) 404-366-9400

- Dictator Records
  4065 Memorial Dr., Suite D, Decatur, GA 30032
  P) 404-412-1111

- Discolandia Record Shops (8)
  3352 Buford Hwy, Atlanta, GA 30329
  P) 404-417-0506

- Dolphin Music Distributors
  6500 McDonough Dr, Ste A-3, Norcross, GA 30093
  P) 770-368-1808 P) 800-390-5853 F) 800-617-4228
  www.dolphinmusic.com
  info@dolphinmusic.com

- Earwax Records
  565 Spring St., Atlanta, GA 30308
  P) 404-875-5600 F) 404-875-7393
  www.earwaxrecords.com
  earwax1@bellsouth.net

- Ella Guru
  2993 N. Druid Hills Road, Atlanta, GA 30329
  P) 404-325-1350
  don@mindspring.com

- E-Music
  2020 Eastside Dr., Suite 203, Conyers, GA 30013
  P) 678-413-4803 P) 770-366-8107

- FYE-North Point Mall
  2208 N Point Cir., Alpharetta, GA 30022
  P) 770-664-5751

- FYE-Lenox Square Mall
  3393 Peachtree Rd NE Ste 2017, Atlanta, GA 30326
  P) 404-995-9450

- FYE-Cumberland Mall
  1303 Cumberland Mall SE, Atlanta, GA 30339
  P) 770-432-0036

- FYE-Perimeter Mall
  4400 Ashford Dunwoody Rd NE Ste 2405
  Atlanta, GA 30346
  P) 770-350-0047

- FYE-Augusta Mall
  3450 Wrightsboro Rd Ste 2030, Augusta, GA 30909
  P) 706-736-4500

- FYE-Colonial Mall-Glynn Place, 100 Mall Blvd
  Brunswick, GA 31520
  P) 912-267-6718

- FYE-The Galleria @ Centerville
  2922 Watson Blvd Ste 930, Centerville, GA 31028
  P) 478-953-9666

- FYE-Peachtree Mall
  3507 Manchester Expy Ste 51, Columbus, GA 31909
  P) 706-323-7624

- FYE-North DeKalb Mall
  2050 Lawrenceville Hwy, Decatur, GA 30033
  P) 404-329-0071

- FYE-Arbor Place
  6700 Douglas Blvd Ste 2230, Douglasville, GA 30135
  P) 678-838-0022

- FYE-Gwinnett Place
  2100 Pleasant Hill Rd., Duluth, GA 30096
  P) 770-476-9550

- FYE-Colonial Mall Macon
  3661 Eisenhower Pkwy., Macon, GA 31206
  P) 478-477-8143

- FYE- Southlake Mall
  1114 Southlake Mall, Morrow, GA 30260
  P) 770-968-3998

- FYE-Oglethorpe Mall
  7804 Abercorn St Unit 167, Savannah, GA 31406
  P) 912-692-1200

- FYE- Shannon Mall
  545 Shannon Mall, Union City, GA 30291
  P) 770-306-8511

- FYE- Colonial Mall Valdosta
  1700 Norman Dr Ste 1070, Valdosta, GA 31601
  P) 229-247-3548

- Gospel Express Music
  2472 Martin Luther King Jr. Dr., Atlanta, GA 30311
  P) 404-505-1345

- Gospel Express Music
  2091 Candler Rd., Suite-A, Decatur, GA 30032
  P) 404-288-8055

- Jay's Music
  880 New Hope Rd., Lawrenceville, GA 30045
  P) 770-338-0383 F) 770-338-0033
  www.jaysmusic.biz
  jaythomp64@aol.com

- Jumpstreet Records
  5133 Old National Hwy, College Park, GA 30349
  P) 404-767-4844 F) 404-767-2993
  www.jumpstreetrecords.com
  ljumpin@aol.com

- Lady T's Records
  3897 Glenwood Rd., Decatur, GA
  P) 404-534-0744

- Major Turnout
  625 Lawrence St., Marietta, GA 30060
  P) 770-419-1526 F) 770-419-8544
  majorturnout@mindspring.com

- Mo' Music
  2234 S. Cobb Dr., Smyrna, GA 30080
  P) 678-556-9223
  www.momusicent.com
  momusicent@hotmail.com

- Moods Music
  1130 Euclid Ave., Little 5 Points, Atlanta, GA 30307
  P) 404-653-0724
  www.moodsmusic.net
  info@moodsmusic.net

- Music Media
  2701 Candler Rd., Decatur, GA 30024

P) 404-381-0024

- Music Vibrations
  822 McDonough Blvd., Atlanta, GA 30315
  P) 404-633-1562 F) 404-635-1542

- No Major Music
  486 Decatur St., Decatur, GA 30312
  P) 404-524-8480

- North GA Compact Disc
  515 Beaver Ruin Rd., Norcross, GA 30071
  P) 770-416-6575

- Peppermint Records-South Dekalb Mall
  2801 Candler Rd., Atlanta, GA 30034
  P) 404-243-6300
  southdeklabpep@aol.com

- Reloaded
  82 Peachtree Street, Atlanta, GA 30342
  P) 404-914-1907

- Rebel Musik
  353 Edgewood Ave., Atlanta, GA 30312
  P) 404-584-0780

- Satellite Records
  421 Moreland Ave., Atlanta, GA 30307
  P) 404-880-9746 F) 404-880-0350
  www.satelliterecords.com
  greg@satelliterecords.com

- Schoolkids Records
  264 East Clayton St., Athens, GA 30601
  P) 706-353-1666 F) 706-353-2232
  www.schoolkidsrecords.com
  schoolkidsrecords@earthlink.net

- Sound Shop-West End Mall
  810 Oak St., SW, Atlanta, GA 30310
  P) 404-752-9494

- Super Sound Music
  2740 Greenbriar Pkwy. SW, Suite #9
  Atlanta, GA 30331
  P) 404-349-2969

- Super Sounds Music
  4919 Flatshoals Parkway, Suite 108, Decatur, GA 30034
  P) 770-323-5720 F) 770-323-5279

- Super Sound Music
  79 Price Quarters Rd., McDonough, GA 30080
  P) 678-583-6346

- Time for CD
  3579 Martin Luther King Dr., Atlanta, GA 30331
  P) 404-699-0669

- Top 20 Records
  2524 Bouldercrest Rd., Suite B, Atlanta, GA

- Tower Records
  3232 Peachtree Rd., Atlanta, GA 30305
  P) 404-264-1217
  www.tower.com

- Vibes Music & More
  145-B Sycamore St., Decatur, GA 30030
  P) 404-373-5099
  vibesmusicandmore@earthlink.net

- Wax N' Facts
  432 Moreland Ave., NE, Atlanta, GA
  P) 404-525-2275

- Wuxtry Records
  2096 N. Decatur Road, Decatur, GA. 30033
  P) 404-329-0020 F) 404-248-9679
  www.wuxtryrecords.com
  atlanta@wuxtryrecords.com

- Wuxtry Records
  197 E. Clayton Street, Athens, Georgia 30601
  P) 706-369-9428 F) 706-548-7703

www.wuxtryrecords.com
athens@wuxtryrecords.com

- Low Yo-Yo Stuff
  285 W. Washington St. Athens, GA 30601
  P) 706-227-6199
  www.lowyoyostuff.com

Who tracks and monitors radio airplay?

BDS-(Broadcast Data Service) and Mediabase track radio airplay. Registering a song with BDS and/or Mediabase is important to determine the correct number of spins or times a song is played on commercial radio to insure accurate chart position i.e. Billboard Charts. It should be noted that ASCAP, BMI and SESAC also monitor radio airplay to ensure that their writers and publishers are paid public performance royalties (money).

Media Guide is the newest player on the block providing radio airplay monitoring service for music industry professionals, independent artists and songwriters.

Contacting BDS, Media Guide & Mediabase

- BDS (Broadcast Data Service)
  550 11th St., Suite 201, Miami Beach, FL 33139
  P) 305-777-2371 F) 305-777-2372
  www.bdsonline.com

- Media Guide
  1000 Chesterbrook Blvd. Ste 150, Berwyn, PA 19312
  P) 610-578-0800 F) 610-578-0804
  www.mediaguide.com
  contact@mediaguide.com

- Mediabase
  15260 Ventura Blvd., Ste 1500
  Sherman Oaks, CA, 91403
  P) 818-461-5435 P) 818-461-8657
  www.mediabase.com

COLLEGE & COMMUNITY RADIO

College and Community Radio Stations tend to be more receptive to playing independent or underground music. For this reason it may be of greater benefit to solicit your music to these stations before attempting to get radio airplay from commercial radio stations. In addition, these stations are usually open to an artist scheduling an on-air interview, providing drops or leaving music to be given away to station listeners. All these opportunities should be explored to help increase an artist's fan base and generate more sales.

- 88.5 WRAS
  MSC 8L0377
  Georgia State University, P.O. Box 4048
  Atlanta, GA 30302
  P) 404-651-2240 Request line) 404-651-4488
  www.wras.org

- 89.3 WRFG Radio Free Georgia-Format All
  1083 Austin Ave. NE, Atlanta, GA 30307
  P) 404-523-3471 Request Line) 404-523-8989
  www.wrfg.org
  info@wrfg.org

- 91.1 WREK
  Georgia Tech
  350 Ferst Dr., Suite 2224, Atlanta, GA 30332
  P) 404-894-2468 F) 404-894-6872
  www.wrek.org

- 91.9 WCLK
  Clark Atlanta University
  111 James P. Brawley Dr., SW, Atlanta, GA 30314
  P) 404-880-8273 Request Line) 404-880-9255
  www.wclk.com

- WRME
  Emory University
  PO Drawer AG, Atlanta, GA 30322
  P) 404-727-9672 F) 404-712-8000

COMMERICAL RADIO

Contrary to popular belief commercial radio should be the last stop an independent artist should approach for marketing a new release. Normally, an artist will need deep pockets ($$$) and the right contacts to get any significant radio airplay. For these reasons artist should continue to perfect their craft, grow a loyal fan base and perform every chance they get. After successfully doing this, you may want to retain (hire and/or secure) the services of a professional radio promotions consultant, such as Parrish Johnson, Indie 1st Co-op. Traditionally, a radio promotions consultant, artist and/or label will have a series of meetings with the radio station program/music director in an effort to get a new song played and possibly added to the stations rotation. Because of mergers, acquisitions and corporate restructuring radio stations sometimes change their programming format (the style of music they play), for this reason I have purposely left off the genre of music each station is currently playing.

To ensure you receive royalties (money) when your song is played on radio, you will need to become a writer and publishing member of one of the three performance rights organizations ASCAP, BMI or SESAC. While many new artist leave registering with a performance rights organization up to a manager or consultant it is wise that you do it yourself for several reasons. First, you become familiar with the process. Second, you increase your knowledge base on music publishing i.e. you are forced to read through the PRO's paperwork. Third, by completing and submitting the registration packet yourself, you ensure that you receive proper credit and royalties for songs that you have written, co-written and/or published.

- 860 AM
  1465 Northside Drive, Suite 218, Atlanta, GA 30318

P) 404-355-8600 F) 404-754-1887

- 1160AM WMLB
  1100 Spring St., Suite 610, Atlanta, GA 30309
  P) 404-681-9307 F) 404-659-1329
  www.am1160.net

- 1340AM WALR
  3535 Piedmont Rd. Bldg.14, Suite 1200
  Atlanta, GA 30305
  P) 404-688-0068 F) 404-995-4045

- 1380AM WAOK
  1201 Peachtree St., Colony Square
  Suite 800, Atlanta, GA 30309
  P) 404-898-8900 F) 404-898-8987

- 1430AM WGFS
  1151 Hendricks St., SW, P.O. Box 2419
  Covington, GA 30015
  P) 770-786-1430 F) 770-784-9892

- 1480AM WYZE
  1111 Boulevard SE, Atlanta, GA 30312
  P) 404-622-7802 F) 404-622-6767
  www.wyzeradio.com

- 92.9FM WZGC
  1100 Johnson Ferry Rd NE, Suite 593,
  Atlanta, GA 30342
  P) 404-851-9393 F) 404-843-3541

- 94.1FM WSTR
  3350 Peachtree Rd NE, Suite 1800, Atlanta, GA 30326
  P) 404-261-2970 F) 404-365-9026
  www.star94.com

- 94.9FM WPCH
  1819 Peachtree Rd NE Suite 700, Atlanta, GA 30309
  P) 404-367-0949 F) 404-367-9490

- 96.1FM WKLS
  1819 Peachtree Rd NE Suite 700, Atlanta, GA 30309

P) 404-325-0960 F) 404-367-1156

- 97.5FM WPZE
  101 Marietta St., Atlanta, GA 30303
  P) 404-765-9750
  www.975.com

- 99.7FM WNNX
  780 Johnson Ferry Rd NE, Atlanta, GA 30342
  P) 404-266-0997 F) 404-364-5855
  www.99x.com

- 100.5FM WWWQ
  780 Johnson Ferry Rd, NE, Atlanta, GA 30342
  P) 404-497-4700 F) 404-364-5855
  www.allthehits.com

- 101.5FM WKHX
  210 Interstate North Pkwy SE FL 6, Building 210
  Atlanta, GA 30339
  P) 770-955-0101 F) 770-850-0101

- 102.5FM WAMJ
  101 Marietta St., Atlanta, GA 30303
  P) 404-765-9750 F) 404-688-7686

- 103.3FM WVEE
  1201 Peachtree St., 400 Colony Square, Suite 800
  Atlanta, GA 30361
  P) 404-898-8900 F) 404-898-8987

- 104.1FM WALR
  1201 Peachtree St., 400 Colony Square, Suite 800
  Atlanta, GA 30361
  P) 404-897-7500 F) 404-897-6595

- 107.5FM WJZZ
  101 Marietta St., Atlanta, GA 30303
  P) 404-765-9750 F) 404-688-7686

- 107.9FM WHTA
  101 Marietta St., Atlanta, GA 30303
  P) 404-765-9750 F) 404-688-7686

INTERNET RADIO STATIONS

- www.atlanta11.com/radio.htm
- www.atlantabluesky.com - Blues
- www.digital-djs.com
- www.dr-love.com - Hip Hop, R&B, Neo-Soul
- www.dryerbuzz.com - Hip Hop, R&B, Neo-Soul
- www.liquidsoulradio.com - Neo-Soul, R&B
- www.lodradio.com - Hip Hop, R&B, Crunk
- www.ruleradio.net
- www.urbanindiemusic.com- Hip Hop, R&B, Neo-Soul
- www.xmradio.com - All
- www.web-radio.fm - Locate radio stations

MUSIC & ENTERTAINMENT MAGAZINES

Entertainment and music magazines offer you a fantastic way to create a buzz for your live performance and CD release. It is often easier to get local and regional press interested in your music and doing either a CD review or interview versus trying to get it from a national publication. Here are some steps to getting local magazines interested in you.

First, find out who does CD reviews or interviews at the magazine. Second, send that person a press kit or EPK (electronic press kit)- whichever they prefer. Third, invite that person(s) to see you perform live. Remember to roll out the red carpet for these folks. For instance, make sure that they don't have to pay to get into the venue where you are performing and offer to buy them something to eat or drink that night. Fourth, after the performance thank the person for coming out and leave them alone unless they want to talk to you. Fifth, follow-up with them a few days later via email or by phone and ask the person if there is anything they would improve upon about your performance. Make them feel like they are the most important person in the world.

- Atlanta Talent Magazine
  P.O. Box 28934, Atlanta, GA 30358
  P) 866-853-8539
  www.atlantatalentmagazine.com
  talent@atlantatalentmagazine.com

- Break Magazine
  3535 Peachtree St., Suite 520-335, Atlanta, GA 30326
  P) 404-630-8534 F) 404-745-8070
  www.breakn2.com
  mdtrammell@hotmail.com

- Flagpole
  P.O. Box 1027, Athens, GA 30603
  P) 706-549-9523 F) 706-548-8981
  www.flagpole.com
  music@flagpole.com

- Georgia Music Magazine
  329 Colton Avenue, Macon, GA 31201
  P) 478-744-9955 F) 678-559-0263
  www.georgiamusicmag.com
  info@georgiamusicmag.com

- Gospel Today/Gospel Industry Today
  286 Highway 314, Suite C, Fayetteville, GA 30214
  P) 770-719-4825 F) 770-716-2660
  www.gospeltoday.com
  gospeltodaymag@aol.com

- Grip Magazine
  P.O. Box 475, Stockbridge, GA 30281
  P) 877-474-7624
  www.grpmag.com

- Hip Hop Encounter
  P.O. Box 1133, Experiment, GA 30212
  www.hiphopencounter.com

- Holla Magazine
  P.O. Box 1367, Smyrna, GA 30081
  P) 678-467-9418
  www.hollamag.com

info@hollamag.com

- Insite Magazine
  2250 North Druid Hills Rd., Ste 100, Atlanta, GA 30329
  P) 404-315-8485 F) 404-315-1755
  www.insiteatlanta.com
  feedback@insiteatlanta.com

- Jive Magazine
  P.O. Box 2635, Lilburn, GA 30048
  P) 404-735-2613 F) 801-457-1605
  www.jivemagazine.com
  sales@jivemagazine.com

- Juice Magazine
  P.O. Box 11050, Atlanta, GA 30310
  P) 404-696-0120 P) 877-926-3368 F) 404-696-0171
  www.thejuicemagazine.net

- Look Magazine
  3915 Cascade Rd., Suite T-115, Atlanta, GA 30331
  P) 404-696-4034 Cell) 404-438-5158
  www.lookmag.com
  rjones@lookmag.com

- **MIC (Music Industry Connection)**
  P.O. Box 52682, Atlanta, GA 30355
  P) 800-963-0949
  www.mt101.com

- Playground Magazine
  P.O. Box 8154, Columbus, GA 31907
  P) 706-562-0074
  www.playgroundsmag.com
  playgroundsmag@knology.net

- Rolling Out Urbanstyle Weekly
  257 Spring St. SW., Atlanta, GA, 30303
  P) 404-681-2001 F) 404-475-1122
  www.rollingout.com
  info@rollingout.com

- Southeast Performer
  449 ½ Moreland Ave. #206, Atlanta, GA 30307
  P) 404-582-0088 F) 404-582-0089
  www.performermag.com
  sepeditortial@performermag.com

- Street Masters Magazine
  2221 Peachtree Rd D-107, Atlanta, GA 30309
  P) 404-271-7727
  www.streetmastersmagazine.com
  vwilson@streetmastersmagazine.com

- Stomp & Stammer
  P.O. Box 55233, Atlanta, GA 30308
  P) 706-369-0833 F) 706-369-0218
  www.stompandstammer.com
  mailroom@stompandstammer.com

How To Use Record Pools To Test-Market Your Next Hit

Record pools are DJ Membership organizations that give you cost-effective access to radio, club and mobile DJs. Essentially, DJs pay either a monthly, quarterly or yearly dues to be a record pool member. In exchange for paying membership dues the record pool distributes new music to the DJs in either CD or Vinyl Formats. Normally, the DJs are required to give feedback or listener response to the pool director in a timely fashion. For instance, the DJs may report to the pool director once a week. When the DJs have sent in their feedback reports the pool director compiles a chart list that is distributed to record companies via fax and/or email. The chart list is sent regularly. For instance, it may be sent once a week or twice a month. Record pools are one of the most cost-effective ways to either generate a buzz or monitor a potential hit. It should be noted that record pools tend to work best for styles of music that are played in clubs i.e. Dance, Hip Hop, R&B, Pop and Trip Hop, etc. One of the reasons that there may be a Club or Dance Remix to a song is so it may be played in a nightclub setting.

Many record pools have regular meetings either bi-weekly, monthly or quarterly. Actively attending these meetings is a fantastic way to meet the DJs that can help break your record. By actively participating I mean attending these meetings prepared to network. For instance, make sure that you have business cards, flyers and other promotional material to distribute to everyone at the meeting. I attended the Leaders of Development Record Pool Meeting in Atlanta and was able to give a few copies of my newspaper the **MIC (Music Industry Connection)** to Greg Street. Greg is one of the top radio-personalities in Atlanta, Georgia and Dallas, Texas yet he was very approachable during the meeting. Because record pool meetings are music business events most people are receptive to networking.

It has been my experience that record pool meetings are some of the best places to meet industry tastemakers in your own backyard.

In addition to networking with industry tastemakers in your own backyard, record pool meetings are an excellent way to get immediate response from DJs about your new music. DJs tend to be very honest when giving feedback about new music at these events. Some of the record pool meetings offer live talent showcases for artists to perform in. While sponsorship (paying money) is normally required to perform in the record pool talent showcases it usually is worth the investment to perform in front of the DJs that can help propel your career. **Remember to treat everyone that you meet like they are the most important person on earth.** Not only will this move your career forward faster, but more importantly it will help you have more fun in a cutthroat industry. In addition, you never know whom you may be talking to; it could be a radio station music/program director or editor of a music magazine. This is especially true when you begin attending record pool meetings outside your home market.

Now, let's say that you are an independent record company in Atlanta, Georgia and you're preparing to release a CD. Before spending all your advertising dollars in Atlanta, you will want to test-market your first single using record pools in Georgia, Alabama, South Carolina and Florida. After a few weeks you might find that your single is getting a so-so response in Atlanta, but in Birmingham, Alabama and South Carolina your single has the potential of being this year's summer hit! Since, Birmingham and South Carolina are only a two and three hour drive from Atlanta, respectively, it might make good sense to spend more of your advertising dollars in those areas, remember the How to Promote Your Independent Release Article in the first chapter. This will increase your opportunities for creating a street buzz faster and turning a profit sooner via CD, concert ticket and merchandising sales.

Before spending you hard earned money from your day job pursuing your music career at night, consider record pools as a cost-effective method of test-marketing your next hit. At the end of this book are details on obtaining record pool names, the pool director, the physical mailing address, phone & fax number, website and email address if applicable. The record pool list is available in both print and CD E-Book version in the book *Music Industry Connection: The Truth About Record Pools & Music Conferences by JaWar.* The CD version is great, because it allows you to quickly find record pools across the U.S. either by name or by state and is compatible with Microsoft Excel for PCs. You may order your list of over 130 U.S. Record Pools by completing and mailing in the order-form at the end of this book. Tell the Record Pools & DJ Organizations below you found them in the Atlanta Music Industry Connection Book by JaWar.

RECORD POOLS & DJ ORGANIZATIONS

- Aphilliates, LLC
  P.O. Box 4596, Atlanta, GA 30302
  P) 404-524-1266 F) 404-524-1267
  www.theaphilliates.com

- Atlanta Urban Mix
  131 Walker Street, Suite-B, Atlanta, GA 30313
  P) 404-589-1126 F) 404-589-1127 Cell) 404-966-1847
  www.atlantaurbanmix.com
  msmoak@atlantaurbanmix.com

- Big City DJ's CD-Pool
  4660 Cedar Keys Lane, Stone Mountain, GA 30083
  P) 404-501-0220 Cell) 404-867-9133
  www.bigcitydjs.com
  pooldirector@bigcitydjs.com

- Digital DJs, LLC
  8725 Roswell Rd, Suite O-166, Atlanta, GA 30350
  P) 732-979-3338
  www.digital-djs.com

info@digital-djs.com

- Dixie Dance Kings Record Pool
  42 Milton Ave., Alpharetta, GA 30004
  P) 770-740-0356 P) 770-740-0357 F) 770-740-0358
  www.dancekings.com
  ddkings@aol.com

- Hittmen DJs
  2214 April Lane, Decatur, GA 30035
  P) 404-328-8823
  www.hittmendjs.com
  contact@hittmendjs.com

- Jumpin Jack Record Pool
  970 Park Gate Place, Stone Mountain, GA 30083
  P) 770-413-9339 P) 404-663-1130
  recordpool@go.com
  wali_56@yahoo.com

- **L.O.D. (Legion of Doom) Record Pool**
  5319 Old National Hwy., College Park, GA 30349
  P) 404-684-5898 P) 404-392-9415 F) 404-684-5973
  www.lodrecordpool.com
  info@lodrecordpool.com

- Majestic Latin Music Pool
  3689 Hermitage Drive, Duluth, GA 30096
  P) 770-622-2565
  latinmusicpool@yahoo.com

- Million Dollar Record Pool
  2459 Roosevelt Hwy., Ste B-1 College Park, GA 30337
  P) 404-766-1275 F) 404-559-0117
  www.mildol.com
  mde@mildol.com

How are CD sales tracked? What is Soundscan?

CDs sold through music retail stores are normally tracked by Sound Scan. A CD must contain a U.P.C. Barcode, must be registered with Sound Scan and the retail store must be a Sound Scan reporting store before the CD will be tracked through the Sound Scan System.

Having a CD tracked through Sound scan is wonderful if you are interested in getting chart position through Billboard or getting the attention of a major record company or distributor. However, if you simply want to sell your CDs, make a profit and keep it moving- you don't need Sound scan. There are plenty of people making a decent living or extra money from selling CDs that are not being tracked through the Sound scan System. For instance, they sell their music through the Internet, at their live performances and out the trunk of their cars and backpacks.

How do I ensure proper credit for my CD sales?

- Contact SoundScan Client Services
  One North Lexington Avenue, Gateway Building, 14 FL
  White Plains, NY 10601
  P) 914-684-5525 F) 914-684-5606
  www.soundscan.com

Does SoundScan track CDs sold at live venues?

Yes, SoundScan tracks CDs sold at live performances.

To track CDs sold at live performances contact

- SoundScan Venue Service
  P) 914-684-5506 F) 914-686-1556
  www.soundscan.com

MARKETERS & PROMOTERS

As you begin to expand your reach, you will need the services of professional radio, retail and street promotions companies that will develop a comprehensive marketing plan that you can execute.

Before contacting the companies below, know what you are seeking. For instance, you may want to get commercial or college radio airplay for your next single. In addition, you may seek to promote your new release to a certain demographic (e.g. Asian females between the ages of 21 and 35.) Also know what your budget is for a particular promotions campaign. For example, you may have a $500 budget for national street promotions. At that point the promoter will undoubtedly tell you that $500 want be enough for a national street promotions campaign, but you may get the word out about your release locally.

Knowing what you hope to accomplish, the time frame you would like to accomplish it in and what your budget is for a particular promotions campaign will save you time and money. In addition, people will take you more seriously in the music business.

Below is list of companies that will help you achieve your goals and realize your potential by branding and promoting your company, artist or band. Remember to tell the companies below that you found them in the Atlanta Music Industry Connection Book by JaWar.

- 911 Promotions
  132 Adair Ave., Atlanta, GA 30315
  P) 404-246-8342 F) 404-287-3500
  ninepromo@yahoo.com

- Big Picture Media
  370 Peachtree Hills Ave., Suite 32, Atlanta, GA 30305
  P) 404-668-0696 F) 940-991-0274
  www.yourbigpicture.com
  tony@yourbigpicture.com

- Coming Attractions Promotions
  2375 Wesley Chapel Rd., Suite 3-1118
  Decatur, GA 30035
  P) 404-886-4650
  arlindamay@aol.com

- Crazy 8 Promotions
  2870 Peachtree Road #442, Atlanta, GA 30305
  P) 718-486-9117
  www.crazy8promotions.com
  jbailey@crazy8promotions.com

- Da Real Hometeam, Inc.
  P.O. Box 1973, Atlanta, GA 30301
  P) 678-508-9274
  www.darealhometeam.com
  info@darealhometeam.com

- Driven Marketing Group
  2826 Summit Ridge Drive, Marietta, GA. 30066
  P) 770-421-9300 F) 770-421-9006
  www.drivenmarketing.com

- GG Promotions
  655 Lambert Drive, Atlanta, GA 30324
  P) 404-425-4388 F) 404-253-6170
  gngpromotions@netzero.com

- Glo Hunter
  Specializes in National Retail Promotions
  208 Vinings Forest Circle, Smyrna, GA 30380
  P) 770-436-7459

- Glue
  3999 Austell Rd, Suite 303-366, Austell, GA 30106
  P) 404-869-0078

- High Profile Music
  P.O. Box 90364, Atlanta, GA 30364-0364
  P) 404-572-9177
  highprofilemusic@yahoo.com

- Jerome Marketing & Promotions
  2535 Winthrope Way, Lawrenceville, GA 30044
  P) 770-982-7055 F) 770-982-1882
  www.jeromepromotions.com
  hitcd@bellsouth.net

- Kreme Marketing

159 Walker St., Atlanta, GA 30310
P) 404-734-3489 P) 404-522-2260 F) 404-522-2270
www.krememarketing.com
philpascal@krememarketing.com

- **Lady Di/Bar Red Entertainment Group**
  P.O. Box 281, Rex, GA 30273
  P) 770-912-8065 P) 770-931-2945 F) 770-931-2226
  www.ldbr-entgrp.com
  info@ldbr-entgrp.com

- Marketing Works
  1270 W. Peachtree St., NW, Ste 17E, Atlanta, GA 30309
  P) 404-272-3956
  msdionne03@yahoo.com

- New Step Promotions
  989 Pointer Ridge, Tucker, GA 30084
  P) 678-596-7015 P) 404-547-9861
  www.newsteppromotions.com
  newsteppromo@yahoo.com

- Real Street Promotions
  1440 Dutch Valley Pl, Suite-700 Atlanta, GA 30324
  P) 404-685-8996 F) 404-685-1678
  www.realstreetpromo.com
  info@realstreetpromo.com

- Shimon Presents, Inc.
  126 Terrace Dr. NE Apt-D., Atlanta, GA 30305
  P) 404-467-8520
  www.shimonpresents.com
  shimoner@gmail.com

- Sixthman
  158 Moreland Ave., SE, Atlanta, GA 30316
  P) 404-525-0222 F) 404-525-0225
  www.sixthman.net

- Spectrum
  5028, Thompson Mill Rd., Lithonia, GA 30038
  P) 770-808-8596 F) 770-808-6935
  spectrumali@mindspring.com

- Team Clermont
  191 East Broad St., Suite 310, Athens, GA 30601
  P) 706-548-6008 F) 706-548-0094
  www.teamclermont.com
  decisionmakers@teamclermont.com

- Urban Edge Entertainment
  207 Monterey Pkwy., Atlanta, GA 30350
  P) 404-514-5849
  www.urbanedgeentertainment.com
  urbanedge_ent@yahoo.com

- Wicked Group
  659 Auburn Ave, NE, Suite 248, Atlanta, GA 30312
  P) 404-589-9888 F) 404-589-0802
  www.wickedgroup.com
  info@wickedwestpr.com

- VIS Studio
  659 Auburn Ave., #258, Atlanta, GA 30312
  P) 404-221-0015 F) 404-221-1183
  www.studiovis.com
  ephelps@studiovis.com

INTERNET RESOURCE GUIDE

- www.atlantamusicguide.com
- www.atlantamusician.com
- www.atlantashows.org
- www.georgiabands.com
- www.slabmusic.com
- www.soopastar.com
- www.wholeteam.com

GRAPHIC DESIGN COMPANIES

- Alexxus Graphics
  625 Lawrence St., Marietta, GA 30060
  P) 770-419-1526 F) 770-419-8544
  majorturnout@mindspring.com

- Blaze 1 Graphixs
  4548 Howell Farms Rd., Acworth, GA 30303
  P) 770-975-0522
  www.blaze1graphixs.com

- Eboni Graphix
  3350 Riverwood Parkway, Suite 1900
  Atlanta, GA 30339
  P) 678-354-9078 F) 678-354-3997
  www.eboni-graphix.com
  lbeverly@eboni-graphix.com

- Green Designs
  5744 Norman Ct., College Park, GA 30349
  P) 404-388-6888 F) 770-991-0120
  www.greendesigns.org
  tgreen@greendesigns.org

- I Design Graphics
  4600 Cascade Rd., Atlanta, GA 30331
  P) 404-505-1443 F) 404-691-5209
  www.ithanpaynecreative.com
  ithanpayne@aol.com

- Image Evolutions
  1152 Woodmere Dr., Suite 100, Lithonia, GA 30058
  P) 770-484-6554 F) 801-601-0053
  www.imageevolutions.com
  info@imageevolutions.com

- Jamire
  P.O. Box 492494, College Park, GA 30349
  P) 866-629-3475 P) 404-403-2729
  www.jamire.com
  tcarpenter@jamire.com

- Master Mind Graphics, LLC
  20 Executive Park Drive, Ste. 2002, Atlanta, GA 30329
  P) 404.529.9937 P) 404.320.6175
  www.mm-graphics.com
  info@mm-graphics.com

- Moz Graphics

3334 Sable Run Rd., College Park, GA 30349
P) 404-849-3220
www.mozgraphics.com
moz@mozgraphics.com

- Sigmoe Media Group
  1715 Jasmine Circle Unite 18103, Atlanta, GA 30315
  P) 404-849-1157
  www.sigmoemediagroup.com
  cedric@sigmoemediagroup.com

- Star Shooters Atlanta
  277-B East Paces Ferry Rd, Atlanta, GA 30305
  P) 404-869-8844 F) 404-869-8833

MUSIC CONSULTANTS

- Embacy Entertainment
  P.O. Box 87396, Atlanta, GA 30337
  P) 404-272-0763 F) 512-485-2198
  info@embacyentertainment.com

- Entertainment Business Consultant
  3075-H Colonial Way, Chamblee, GA 30341
  P) 404-290-1888
  www.entertainmentbizlink.com
  ngowens@gmail.Com

- Incognito Entertainment
  P.O. Box 311880, Atlanta, GA 31131
  P) 404-405-3078
  www.incognitoent.com
  mikesublett@incognitoent.com

- Indie 1st Entertainment Co-op
  2870 Peachtree Rd., Suite 425, Atlanta, GA 30305
  P) 404-521-2000 F) 404-521-2040
  www.indie1st.com
  parrish@indie1st.com

- Music Industry Connection
  P.O. Box 52682, Atlanta, GA 30355
  P) 800-963-0949
  www.mt101.com
  questions@mt101.com

- Right Path Industry Consultants
  8622 Glendevon Ct., Riverdale, GA 30274
  P) 404-427-0477 F) 770-471-9631
  www.rightpathconsultant.com
  Carl@rightpathconsultant.com

- Seven Diamond Foundation
  P.O. Box 16806, Atlanta, GA 30321
  P) 770-572-0700 P) 404-899-3299
  www.startyourrecordlabel.com
  Se7en@startyourrecordlabel.com

- The Artist Factory
  1741 Commerce Dr., Atlanta, GA 30318
  P) 404-352-0404 F) 404-352-0405
  www.artistfactory.com
  info@artistfactory.com

- Xavier Entertainment
  Contact: Mose Hardin
  6980 Roswell Rd., D-11, Atlanta, GA 30328
  P) 888-661-8242 P) 678-598-1280
  www.xavierentertainment.net
  mose@xavierentertainment.net

MUSIC ORGANIZATIONS

- Afar Music
  P.O. Box 161950, Atlanta, GA 30321
  P) 770-969-6522
  www.afarmusic.com
  mayo_jon@afarmusic.com

- AFM-Atlanta Federation of Musicians
  551 Dutch Valley Road NE, Atlanta, GA 30324
  P) 800-854-5178 P) 404-873-2033 F) 404-873-0019
  www.atlantamusicians.com
  ac@atlantamusicians.com

- ASCAP
  American Society of Composers, Authors and Publishers
  PMB-400, 541 10th Street NW, Atlanta, GA 30318
  P) 404-351-1224
  www.ascap.com

- BMI-Broadcast Music, Inc.
  P.O. Box 19199, Atlanta, GA 31126
  P) 404-261-5151 F) 404-261-5152
  www.bmi.com

- GMEA-Georgia Music Educators Association
  P.O. Box 777, Jonesboro, GA 30237
  P) 770-472-4632 F) 770-472-4213
  www.gmea.org

- GMIA-Georgia Music Industry Association
  3063 Clairmont Rd. NE, Atlanta, Georgia 30329
  www.gmia.org

- NABFEME-Atlanta Chapter
  P.O. Box 16112, Atlanta, GA 30321
  P) 404-508-4612
  www.nabfeme.org
  nabfemeatlanta@yahoo.com

- NARAS
  National Academy of Recording Arts and Sciences
  3290 Northside Parkway, Suite 280, Atlanta, GA 30327

P) 404-816-1380 F) 404-816-1390
www.grammy.com
atlanta@grammy.com

- NAL-National Artist League
  50 Peachtree Street NW Loft # 701 Atlanta, GA 30303
  P) 404-681-0154
  www.nalgear.com
  nal@nalgear.com

- SECUR-Southeast Coalition of Urban Retailers
  Contact: Monique Smith
  1188 Richard Rd., Decatur, GA 30032
  P) 404-288-1590

- SOFRAS
  Society of Future Recording Artists & Songwriters
  P.O. Box 930274, Norcross, GA 30003-0274
  P) 770-281-7286 P/F) 866-442-1926
  www.sofras.net

- Southern Arts Federation
  1800 Peachtree St., NW, Suite 808, Atlanta, GA 30309
  P) 404-874-7244 F) 404-873-2148
  www.southarts.org

- Southeast Organization of Jazz Arts
  P.O. Box 5825, Atlanta, GA 30307
  soja_ga@msn.com

ENTERTAINMENT ATTORNEYS

- K5 Keniley Law Firm, LLC
  4610 Peachtree Industrial Blvd, Norcross, GA 30071
  P) 404-933-1157 F) 404-420-2260
  www.k5law.com
  Scott@k5law.com

- Beitchman & Hudson
  Contact: Lee B. Beitchman or Herman Hudson
  215 Fourteenth Street, NW, Atlanta, GA 30318
  P) 404-897-5252 F) 404-897-5677
  www.arts-entertainmentlaw.com
  Hudson@arts-entertainmentlaw.com

- Bernie Lawrence-Watkins, Esq.
  4070 Laurel Ridge Tr., Smyrna, GA 30080
  P) 770-444-3998 F) 770-444-9599

- Brison & Associates, LLC
  2100 DeFoors Ferry Rd., #2025, Atlanta, GA 30318
  P) 404-931-3391
  nbrison@comcast.net

- Brock, Clay & Calhoun, P.C.
  49 Atlanta St., Marietta, GA 30060
  P) 770-422-1776 F) 770-426-6155
  brockclay.com

- Charles J. Driebe Jr.
  6 Courthouse Wy, Jonesboro, GA 30236
  P) 770-478-8894 F) 770-478-9606

- Clarke & Anderson
  3355 Lenox Rd., Suite 750, Atlanta, GA 30326-1332
  P) 404-816-9800 F) 404-816-0555

- Cliff Lovette, Esq.
  1800 Peachtree St., NW, Atlanta, GA 30309
  P) 404-355-9000 F) 404-475-0680
  cliff.lovette@lovettegroup.com

- Cohen, Cooper, Estep & Mudder, LLC

3350 Riverwood Parkway, Suite 2220,
Atlanta, GA 30339
P) 404-814-0000 F) 404-816-8900
www.coco-law.tv

- Cherry & Cherry, LLC
  Veda V. Cherry
  383-A Ralph McGill Blvd., Atlanta, GA 30312
  P) 404-880-9262 F) 404-880-0897
  Vedavc1@aol.com

- Dante Marshall, Esq.
  1970 Cliff Valley Wy, Suite 250, Atlanta, GA 30329
  P) 404-320-5212 F) 404-320-5214
  D_marshall@dmentertainmentgroup.com

- Drew M. Jackson
  P) 404-609-9885

- Ewing & Roseberry
  6323 Roosevelt Hwy., Union City, GA 30291
  P) 678-325-5402 F) 678-325-5401
  monicaewingesq@mindspring.com

- Gate City Bar Association
  Post Office Box 1921, Atlanta, GA 30301-1921
  www.gatecitybar.org

- Georgia Lawyers for the Arts
  877 W. Marietta St. NW Suite J-101, Atlanta, GA 30318
  P) 404-873-3911
  gla@glarts.org

- Greenberg Taurig Atlanta, LLP
  The Forum
  3290 Northside Pkwy., Suite 400, Atlanta, GA 30327
  P) 678-553-2100 F) 678-553-2212

- Hewitt, Katz, Stepp & Wright
  Contact: Leron E. Rogers
  Resurgens Plaza, Suite 2610
  945 East Paces Ferry Road, Atlanta, GA 30326
  P) 404-240-0400 F) 404-240-0401

leron.rogers@mindspring.com

- Holland & Knight LLP
  One Atlantic Center
  1201 W. Peachtree St, NE, Ste 2000, Atlanta, GA 30309
  P) 404-817-8500 F) 404-881-0470

- **John F. Christmas Entertainment & Sports Attorney**
  P.O. Box 615, Union City, GA 30291
  P) 770-374-8294 F) 770-306-0664
  jochristm@aol.com

- Jonathan E. Leonard, P.C.
  King Plow Arts Center
  949 W. Marietta St., NW, Ste X-102, Atlanta, GA 30318
  P) 404-892-2001 F) 404-892-7001
  jleonard@jellaw.net

- Joseph Arrington II Esq.
  1201 Peachtree St., 400 Colony Sq., Suite 200
  Atlanta, GA 30361
  P) 404-870-9082
  jarringtonII@hotmail.com

- Law Offices of Sidney A. Robbins, LLC
  P.O. Box 4079, Atlanta, GA 30302
  P) 404-589-3595 F) 404-589-3594
  srobbinsa@aol.com

- Lopes McKamey-Lopes
  44 Broad St., NW, Suite 501, Atlanta, GA 30303
  P) 404-589-9000 F) 404-832-4120
  firm@lopesmckameylopes.com

- Marvin S. Arrington, Jr.
  775 Houston Mill Rd, Suite #4, Atlanta, GA 30329
  P) 404-633-3396 P) 404-402-4361
  www.arringtonlawfirm.com
  marvin@arringtonlawfirm.com

- Myers & Kaplan Intellectual Property Law, LLC
  The 1899 Building, 1899 Powers Ferry Rd, Suite 310
  Atlanta, GA 30339

P) 770-541-7444 P) 866-541-7441 F) 770-541-7448
www.myersiplaw.com

- Neighbors, Lett & Johnson, LLC
  The Candler Building
  127 Peachtree St., Suite 555, Atlanta, GA 30303
  P) 404-653-0881 F) 404-653-1171
  www.neighborslettandjohnson.com
  jlett@neighborslettandjohnson.com

- Nicholson & Associates
  1252 W. Peachtree St., NW, Suite 500
  Atlanta, GA 30309
  P) 404-874-6262

- Omara Harris
  P.O. Box 19199, Atlanta, GA, 31126
  P) 404-409-7354
  gamusiclawyer@aol.com

- Rob Hassett
  990 Hammond Dr., Suite 990, Atlanta, GA 30328
  P) 770-393-0990 F) 770-901-9417
  www.internetlegal.com
  rob@internetlegal.com

- Robert L. Hicks
  1291 Fontaine Ave. SW, Atlanta, GA 30311
  P) 404-753-2820

- Robinson & Morgan
  3355 Peachtree Rd., Suite 500, Atlanta, GA 30326
  P) 404-995-7060 F) 404-995-7001

- Self, Glass & Davis
  The Platinum Tower
  1455 Lincoln Pkwy., Suite 300, Atlanta, GA 30346
  P) 770-563-9300 F) 770-563-9330

- Shuli L. Green
  P.O. Box 2839, Decatur, GA 30031
  P) 404-222-8411
  shuligreen@yahoo.com

- Standford, Fagant & Giolito
  1401 Peachtree St., NE, Suite 238, Atlanta, GA 30309
  P) 404-897-1000 F) 404-897-1990

- Stephanie S. Kika
  8108 Trolley Sqxing NE, Atlanta, GA 30306
  P) 770-664-9262 F) 770-892-2150

- Stokes & Murphy
  3593 Hemphill St., Atlanta, GA 30337
  P) 404-766-0076 F) 404-766-8823
  mail@stokesnmurphy.com

- Vernon Slaughter
  1741 Commerce Drive, Atlanta, GA 30318
  P) 404-355-2755 F) 404-355-2720
  slaughterv@bellsouth.net

- Vince Phillips
  P.O. Box 20084, Atlanta GA 30325
  P) 404-522-8000 F) 404-522-7643

- **Washington Law Firm**
  Contact: Karl Washington
  1353 Cleveland, East Point, GA 30344
  P) 404-768-3963 F) 404-768-3966
  karlwashington@att.net

- Weiznecker, Rose, Mattern & Fisher, P.C.
  1800 Peachtree Street, NW, Suite 620
  Atlanta, GA 30309
  P) 404-365-9799 F) 404-917-0979
  www.wrmflaw.com

VIDEO PRODUCTION COMPANIES

Since, the first printing of the book I have come across a number of artists who have their music in stores, have local radio airplay and are performing regularly and want to add video airplay to their marketing mix.

In addition to getting your video played on T.V. and cable, you may consider webcasting (the Internet) and club video airplay. Webcasting your video allows you to have your video scene 24 hours a day 7 days a week by a global audience. You may offer your video via streaming and download on your own website and through other entertainment sites. Club video airplay is when you ask the local club owner, manager or VJ (video-jock) to play your video on the club monitors. Currently most independent artists are not taking full advantage of these opportunities.

A video may cost between a few thousand to millions of dollars to create. To get a video produced for a few thousand dollars, you will either have to shoot it yourself, hire some film students and/or barter (trade) services with another company. In addition to getting a video made and played, you may consider shooting a commercial for your new release.

A commercial may be a cost-effective way of getting your music scene and heard on a regular basis. For instance, you could give DVDs of your commercial to folks that have TV's in their cars and trucks. You could also ask music retail stores to play your commercial in their store where your music is being sold. You may also bring a small monitor and DVD player to industry trade-shows, open mics, talent showcases and music conferences in order to allow potential clients to see and hear your music through your commercial.

Before contacting the video production companies below, know what you want your production to accomplish visually. Also be prepared to discuss your video production budget. For example, let them know that you are seeking to get either a music video or commercial done. You should have ideas for the video or commercial written down. Let them know what your budget is and they will tell you if they can give you what you are looking for. Many times editing is the most time-consuming and expensive part of creating a music video. Tell the video-production companies you found them in the Atlanta Music Industry Connection Book by JaWar.

- 7th Wave Pictures, Inc.
  1208 Woodland Ave., NE, Atlanta, GA 30324
  P) 404-246-9674
  mattruggles1@yahoo.com

- AGORA TV
  Contact: Joe Gora
  195 Hicks Drive, SE, Marietta, GA 30060
  P) 678-581-3750
  www.agoratv.tv
  joe@agoratv.tv

- Antone Productions Services
  644 Antone St., Atlanta, GA 30318
  P) 404-351-3211 F) 404-355-2287
  www.abracadabravideo.com

- Art Visual
  P.O. Box 1003, Pine Lake, GA 30072
  P) 404-292-7727
  www.art-visual.tv
  info@art-visual.tv

- Atlanta Mediaworks
  550 Paris Drive, Lawrenceville, GA 30043
  P) 678-376-7386 Cell) 404-242-7087
  jstovall@atlamediaworks.com

- Atlanta Urban Media Makers
  P.O. Box 50435, Atlanta, GA 30302
  P) 404-460-2793

www.urbanmediamakers.com
aumai@urbanmediamakers.com

- Armcor Productions, Inc.
  P.O. Box 82123, Conyers, GA 30013
  P) 678-333-8127 F) 678-625-1892
  www.positivethemovie.com
  Ralph@positivethemovie.com

- Cely Communications
  3592 Cherokee Road, NE, Atlanta, GA 30340
  P) 770-936-9851
  www.cely.com
  don@cely.com

- Chez Creative, Inc.
  Contact: Deborah E. Harrison
  3588 Hwy. 138 S.E., #266, Stockbridge, GA 30281
  P) 770-478-6226 F) 770-478-8845
  Chez1c@aol.com

- ClipGloss Productions, LLC
  3415 September Morn, Norcross, Georgia 30092
  Cell) 404-518-0688 F) 770-797-3938
  www.clipglossproductions.com
  chris@clipglossproductions.com

- Creative Digital Group
  1888 Emery St., NW, Atlanta, GA 30318
  P) 404-267-7600 F) 404-267-7625
  www.creativedigitalgroup.com

- DanmcCain Productions
  4459-D Abbotts Bridge Rd., Duluth, GA 30097
  P) 770-853-2909
  www.danmccainproductions.com

- DTF
  P.O. Box 4458, Atlanta, GA 30302
  P) 678-558-8526
  deontfranklin@hotmail.com

- DV Illusions
  1486 Mecaslin Street, NW, Atlanta, GA 30309
  P) 404-873-6283 P) 888-7-4-DVI F) 404-873-6409
  www.dvillusions.com
  info@dvillusions.com

- Elevation Sound Motion
  905 Bernina Ave, Atlanta, GA 30307
  P) 404-221-1705 P) 800-813-2214
  www.elevate.tv
  julia@elevate.tv

- EMB Filmworks
  Contact: Edford M. Banuel
  1962 Spectrum Circle, Suite 260, Marietta, GA 30067
  P) 770-514-1406
  embfilmworks@aol.com

- Ess Video
  416 Misty Hollow Road #8226, Ellijay, GA 30536
  P) 770-798-9888
  www.essvideo.com
  mikehein@essvideo.com

- Eye Kiss Films
  660 Ninth St., Suite E, Atlanta, GA 30318
  P) 404-872-1654 F) 404-872-5377
  www.eyekissfilms.com
  questions@eyekissfilms.com

- Focus of Video
  470 Stone Mill Trail, Atlanta, GA 30328
  P) 404-257-0262
  ebrent@peoplepc.com

- Folks Creative
  4249 Courtside Dr., Stone Mountain, GA 30083
  P) 404-932-5760
  jadarenee@yahoo.com

- Forrester Media, Inc.
  3350 Riverwood Pkwy., Suite 1900, Atlanta, GA 30339
  P) 770-420-0762 F) 770-420-0769

www.forrestermedia.com
solutions@forrestermedia.com

- Gold Thread Video Productions
  500 Williams Dr., #213, Marietta, GA 30066
  P) 678-594-7587
  www.goldthread.com
  info@goldthread.com

- Group Communications
  644 Antone Street, Suite 7X, Atlanta, GA 30318
  P) 404-636-9076 P) 888-932-9473 F) 404-367-0928
  www.groupcommunications.com

- Guerrilla le Femme Productions
  630 Woodcrest Manor Dr., Stone Mountain, GA 30083
  P) 404-292-7338 Cell) 404-819-6976
  demetira@tmail.com

- Halestorm Digital Communications
  2440 Krystle Way, Cumming, GA 30041
  P) 678-513-4800 Cell) 678-777-5470
  www.halestormdigital.com
  dhales007@mindspring.com

- Holy Hill Productions
  P.O. Box 312202, Atlanta, GA 31131
  P) 404-691-3307 Cell) 678-595-0995
  www.holyhillproductions.com
  info@holyhillproductions.com

- ImageArts
  1355 Terrell Mill Rd, Building 1472, Suite 200
  Marietta, Georgia 30067
  P) 770-989-0009 F) 770-989-0004
  www.atlanta-imagearts.com

- ImageMaster Productions
  828 Ralph McGill Boulevard NE, Suite W-8
  Atlanta, GA, 30306
  P) 404-231-3200 F) 404-523-7874
  www.imagemaster.tv
  info@imagemaster.tv

- Image Quest Films
  145 Church Street, Suite 140, Marietta, GA 30060
  P) 770-425-2555 V) 888-259-0576
  www.imagequestfilms.com
  imagequest@mindspring.com

- LiJit Pictures
  Contact: Todd Schaffer
  P.O. 94542, Atlanta, GA 30377
  www.lijitpictures.com
  todd@lijitpictures.com

- Magic Eye Productions
  193 Taft St., SW, Atlanta, GA 30315
  magiceye@bellsouth.net

- Malice Films
  2928 Arbor Pl, Decatur, GA 30034
  P) 404-284-0523

- Jumo Mecca Entertainment Group, LLC
  2745 Evergreen Crossing, Dacula, GA 30019
  P) 770-826-2100 P) 770-909-7139
  www.meccamotionpictures.com
  jumo@tmail.com

- Omega Media Group
  3100 Medlock Bridge Road, Suite 100
  Norcross, GA 30071
  P) 770-449-8870 F) 770-449-5463
  www.omegamediagroup.com

- One Edge of A Dream
  1740 Hudson Bridge Rd., Suite 1084
  Atlanta, GA 30281
  P) 678-794-3452
  onedgeofadream@aol.com

- OneFourTwo
  1360 Powers Ferry Road, Suite B110
  Marietta, GA 30067
  P) 770-541-1952 F) 770-541-1953
  www.onefourtwo.com

office@onefourtwo.com

- Partners Video Shop, LTD
  1405 Ralph D. Abernathy Blvd., Atlanta, GA 30310
  P) 404-755-7235 P) 678-698-9354

- Photo Video Connection
  1085 Grace Dr., Lawrenceville, GA 30043
  P) 770-932-0626 Cell) 404-402-2656
  potter_re@bellsouth.net

- Plan B Productions
  1440 Dutch Valley Place, Suite 105, Atlanta, GA 30324
  P) 404-881-8878
  www.planbproductions.com
  info@planbproductions.com

- Power Vision Productions
  P.O. Box 1022, Winder, GA 30680
  P) 770-867-4722 F) 770-307-1465
  www.pvpstudio.com
  info@pvpstudio.com

- Primary Pictures
  1820 Briarwood Industrial Court, Atlanta, GA 30329
  P) 404-321-7900 F) 404-320-0005
  www.primarypictures.com
  info@primarypictures.com

- Pro Media Atlanta, LLC
  1731 Pryor Road #105, Atlanta, GA 30315
  P) 404-281-6771
  www.promediaatlanta.com
  becky@promediaatlanta.com

- Real 2 Real Studios
  7815 Old Morrow Rd., Jonesboro, GA 30236
  P) 770-472-4747 F) 770-472-2371
  www.reellife.net

- R.V. & R Video Productions
  P.O. Box 371737, Atlanta, GA 30037
  P) 404-241-4191

www.rvrvideoproductions.com

- Sharp Eye Video & Photography
  P.O. Box 2583, Decatur, GA 30031
  P) 678-613-1001 P) 770-723-7211

- Sky Film Works
  P.O. Box 666354, Marietta, GA 30066
  P) 678-498-4019
  www.skyfilmworks.com

- Video Atlanta
  5001 LAvista Rd., Tucker, GA 30084
  P) 404-388-9529
  www.videoatlanta.com
  info@videoatlanta.com

- Video Craft Productions
  4325 Settingdown Cir., Suite 101, Cumming, GA 30040
  P) 866-290-2389 F) 866-290-2982
  www.videocraftproductions.com
  info@videocraftproductions.com

- VideoShoots.net LLC
  812 E. Morningside Dr., Atlanta, GA 30324
  P) 404-888-9788 P) 404-247-3456 F) 404-806-6123
  www.musicvideoshoots.com
  info@videoshoots.net

- Wide Open Pictures
  6070 Robbs Crossing Dr., Cumming, GA 30041
  P) 404-215-9685 F) 404-215-8684
  www.wideopenpictures.com

- Whatz Happenin TV
  1529 Springs Rd., Suite-E, Smyrna, GA 30080
  P) 770-437-0002 P) 866-942-8088 F) 770-319-6694
  www.whtv1.com
  sales@whtv1.com

MUSIC VIDEO SHOWS

Below is a list of cable/tv shows that either interview independent artist and/or play their music videos. This is a fantastic way to increase exposure for yourself or band and is wonderful for adding to your bio. Remember to contact the shows for video submission formats and securing an interview. You will also want to find out where the shows are broadcast to ensure that your music is available in local music retail stores in that area prior to your show airing. In addition, have your website up and running so you can let people know where to get details on where your next performances are being held and how they may stay in touch with you. Keep in mind that the contacts are local to Atlanta, but the tactics may be implemented in any market. Wearing a shirt that displays your website in BIG BOLD letters while on a video show is a great way to brand and drive traffic to your website. Remember to tell the folks that you found them in JaWar's Atlanta Music Industry Connection Book.

- Community Showcase: The Talent Zone
  P.O. Box 1994, Stone Mountain, GA 30086
  P) 770-879-9970 F) 770-879-5315
  www.communityshowcase.tv
  communityshowcase@comcast.net

- Detail TV
  2870 Peachtree Rd., Suite 446, Atlanta, GA 30305
  P) 770-256-6462
  www.detailtv.com
  ideas@detailtv.com

- Elements of Soul TV-ESTV
  2482 Randall St., Suite-A, Eastpoint, GA 30344
  P) 678-698-3343
  www.esotv.com
  keith_Muhammad@yahoo.com

- Gospel Music Channel
  One Crown Center

1895 Phoenix Blvd., Suite 355, Atlanta, GA 30349
P) 770-969-7936
www.gospelmusicchannel.com

- Hip Hop Encounter Media
  P.O. Box 1133, Experiment, GA 30212
  P) 770-912-7249

- IMR-Independent Music Revue
  659 Auburn Ave., Suite 147, Atlanta, GA 30312
  P) 404-221-1165
  www.imrtv.com
  info@imrtv.com

- Mainstream Most Wanted
  5475 Memorial Dr., Stone Mountain, GA 30083
  P) 770-912-4000
  www.mainstreammostwanted.com

- Street Eyez Live
  2451 Cumberland Pkwy., Ste 3543, Atlanta, GA 30339
  P) 678-309-9929
  www.streeteyezlive.com
  shadow@streeteyezlive.com

- WHTV 1
  1529 Springs Rd., Suite E, Smyrna, GA 30080
  P) 770-437-0002 P) 866-942-8088 F) 770-319-6694
  www.whtv1.com
  sales@whtv1.com

MUSIC BUSINESS BOOKS

- 100 Miles To A Record Deal
  by Bronson Herrmuth
  www.iowahomegown.com

- Everything You'd Better Know About the Recording
  Industry By Kashif
  kashif@pacificnet.net

- How to Get Paid from the Record Game
  By Raheem
  P) 678-508-3897
  Rah4life@bellsouth.net
  www.tight2defrecords.com

- Official Contact Pages to the Music Business
  5441 Rivderdale Rd., #129, College Park, GA 30349
  P) 404-246-6496 F) 770-478-5553
  www.musiccontactpages.com
  bulletent4000@yahoo.com

- Making It In The Music Business: The Insider Secretes
  By Campbell, Waters, Allen

- Music Powers: To Succeed In The Music Industry
  P.O. Box 9455, Marietta, GA 30065
  P) 770-652-0462
  www.musicpowers.com
  info@musicpowers.com or musicpowers@aol.com

- The Record Game Can Be a Dirty Game
  By Raheem

ATLANTA CLUBS & VENUES

Apache Café
64 3rd St., NW, Atlanta, GA 30308
P) 404-876-5436
www.apachecafe.info

Andres Upstairs
56 East Andres Drive, Suite 13, Atlanta, GA 30305
P) 404-467-1600

Café 290
290 Hildebrand Rd., Atlanta, GA
P) 404-256-3942

Callanwolde Fine Arts Center
980 Briarcliff Rd., Atlanta, GA, 30306
P) 404-872-5338
www.callanwolde.org

Chastain Park Amphitheatre
4469 Stella Dr, Sandy Springs, GA
P) 404-733-4800

Club Eleven 50
1150 Peachtree St., Atlanta, GA 30309
P) 404-874-0428
www.eleven50.com

Club 112
Peachtree St., Atlanta, GA
P) 404-607-7277 F) 404-892-3830
www.club112atl.com

Earthlink Live
1374 West Peachtree St, Midtown, Atlanta, GA 30309
P) 404-885-1365
www.earthlinklive.com

Endenu Restaurant
393 Marietta St, Atlanta, GA 30313
P) 404-522-8874
www.endenu.com

Ferst Center of The Arts
349 Ferst Dr, Atlanta, GA 30332
P) 404-894-9600

House of Blues
1374 West Peachtree St, Atlanta, GA 30309
P) 404-885-1163
www.earthlinklive.com

MJQ Concourse
736 Ponce De Leon Ave, Midtown, GA
P) 404-870-0575
www.mjqatlanta.com

Northside Tavern
1058 Howell Mill Rd, Atlanta, GA, 30318
P) 404-874-8745
www.northsidetaver.com

Smiths Olde Bar
1578 Piedmont Ave. Atlanta, GA, 30324
P) 404-875-1522

The Arena, the Gwinnett Center
1775 Pleasant Hill Rd @ Crestwood, Duluth GA 30096
P) 770-923-1775

The Atrium
5479 Memorial Dr, Stone Mountain, GA

The Fox Theatre
600 Peachtree St, Atlanta, GA
P) 404-249-6400

The Masquerade
695 North Ave, Atlanta, GA 30308
P) 404-577-8178
www.masq.com

The Roxy
3110 Roswell Rd, Atlanta, GA
P) 404-233-ROXY

The Tabernacle
152 Luckie St, Atlanta, GA 30303
P) 404-659-9022

Variety Playhouse
1099 Euclid Ave, Little 5 Points
Atlanta, GA

Visionz
Peachtree Rd., Atlanta, GA

CREATING WEALTH

Whether you earn an additional $5,000 or $5,000,000 a year from the business of music, remember to always put a percentage of your earnings (money that you make) aside, preferably in a tax-sheltered account and invest your money in businesses that have nothing to do with the music industry. This is called diversification of your assets (money). In addition, **you want to always pay yourself first**, spend less money than you earn, carry little to no consumer debt and keep accurate and complete records of the money you earn and spend. This will increase your chances for long-term wealth creation and retention. **Educate yourself about business and money; after all if you don't mind your business and money, someone else will.** To ensure you advance your own learning on saving, investing and creating wealth I have listed a few terms below that you should know.

401(k)
Annuities
Assets
Asset Allocation
Bonds
- Corporate
- Convertible
- Government
CD-Certificate Deposit
Checking Account
Compounding Interest
Debt to Income Ratio
Diversification
Dollar-Cost Averaging
Earnings
Equity
Financial Freedom
Index Funds
Inflation
Investment Portfolio

IRA-Individual
Retirement Account
Keoghs
Market Index
Money-Market Accounts
Money Market Mutual
Funds
NAV (Net Asset Value)
No-Load Mutual Funds
Passive Income
Prospectus
Real Estate
Residual Income
ROI (Return on
Investment)
Roth-IRA, SEP-IRA,
Simple-IRA
Savings Account
Stocks
Tax Sheltered Accounts
Treasury Bills

147

Educate yourself about investing and seek the advice of professionals who may help you verify your information. Publications that may help you become familiar with saving and investing your money are Black Enterprise, The Wall Street Journal, Kiplinger, Money, Smart Money, Barron's, Investor Business Daily, Financial Times, the Business Section of the Atlanta Journal Constitution and the Money Section of USA Today. For more information on saving, investing and making your money grow; visit the following websites.

> www.bankrate.com
> www.blackenterprise.com
> www.buyandhold.com
> www.creditinfocenter.com
> www.fool.com
> www.indexfunds.com
> www.investoreducation.org
> www.jumpstartcoalition.org
> www.kiplinger.com
> www.marketwatch.com
> www.mfea.com
> www.money.com
> www.moneyopolis.org
> www.moringstar.com
> www.richdadpoordad.com
> www.rothira.com
> www.smartmoney.com
> www.tiaacref.com
> www.troweprice.com
> www.youdecide.com
> www.vanguard.com

MUSIC BIZ WORKSHOP

Music Therapy 101

National Music Seminar — mt101.com

Designed by the Music Therapy 101 Marketing Team 800-963-0949

Singers, Rappers, Producers
and Musicians
attend this dynamic seminar
to learn about
the music business & industry.

Attend workshops on
Legal Issues, Marketing & Promotions
Building Your Business, Radio & Retail, etc.,
and the Interactive Activity *How to Press 1,000
Retail Ready CDs Without Using Your Own Money*
presented by JaWar.

Go to **WWW.MT101.COM** for future
Music Therapy 101 dates, times and location

Sponsored by: **KEMETIC RECORDS** www.kemetic.com   Audiovascular Entertainment

For sponsorship and vending opportunities call 800-963-0949 or www.mt101.com

Glossy
Photography.com

678.923.3912

Model and Vocalist: Q   © 2005

DESIGN APART

Urban and Corporate design influences

404_351+4312 (office)
865_385+7778 (direct)
designashil@yahoo.com

album covers
cd inserts/sleeves
logos
business cards
promotional posters
t-shirts
professional photography
fine-arts

"The music business is a bit like life easier when you stick to the fundamentals."

"Do the same thing get the same results, do something different, you might get different results."

Vision
Mission
Team
Opportunity
Drive
Passion
Gratitude
Share
Build
Leadership
Perfection
Helpfulness
Hotep
Wealth
Health
Desire
Win
Rest
Motivate
Cultivate
Feed
Give

Place A Full Page Ad In

(THE MIC)

ATLANTA MUSIC INDUSTRY CONNECTION

contact
800-963-0949
questions@mt101.com

157

SoulWorks
Entertainment

We Manage Music Producers

Landrum Peeples
President/CEO

Phone: 404-808-4979
2978 Rainbow Dr., Suite A #159
Decatur, GA 30034
www.soulworks-ent.com
l_peeples@hotmail.com

When you need original music production or are a music producer seeking
representation/management contact SoulWorks Entertainment.

Force Records

Providing the music industry with entertainment services, including:

Booking
Engineering
Ghostwriting
Graphic Design
Management
Promotions
Production
Songwriting
Studio Recording

Aaron
Brodric
Demetrius
Mygrane
Shawn

theforcepros@yahoo.com

Richard Murray
404-399-0050

Shawn Johnson
404-983-3598

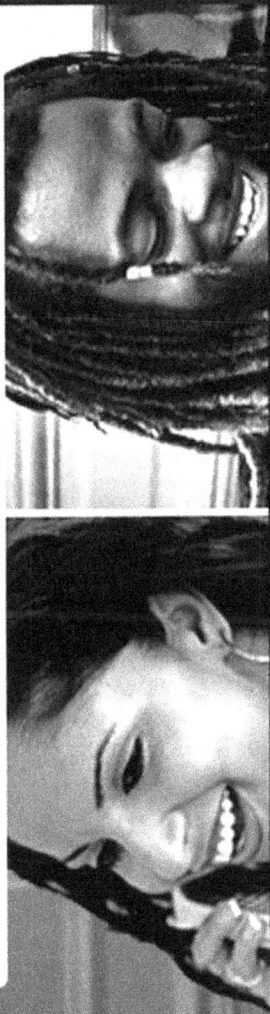

162

163

STREET PRODUCT

"THE MARKETING AND PROMOTIONS SPECIALIST"

CREATE THE HYPE. SHAPE THE OUTCOME.

DO YOU HAVE A PRESENTS IN YOUR CITY?
STREET PRODUCT OFFERS COLLATERAL DISTRIBUTION AND FLYER DISTRIBUTION NATIONALLY IN MOST MAJOR MARKETS ACROSS THE UNITED STATES. STREET PRODUCT AND TASTEMAKERS WORK TO STRATEGICALLY DELIVER YOUR MESSAGE TO CONSUMERS.

FULL STREET TEAM SERVICES

FLYER DISTRIBUTION: WE SYSTEMATICALLY TARGET YOUR PROSPECTIVE CUSTOMERS IN MOTION, AT MAJOR TRAVEL HUBS, WHEREVER THEY MAY GO TO WORK, SHOP, PLAY, SOCIALIZE OR ENTERTAIN.

BUZZ MARKETING: "STREET CREDIBILITY" AND "GRASS ROOTS MARKETING" WHEN PROMOTING LARGE OR SMALL EVENTS.

WE ALSO PROVIDE PROMOTIONAL MODELS AND ARTIST APPEARANCES

POSTER SNIPING:
STREET PRODUCT OFFERS POSTER SNIPING AND OUTDOOR ADVERTISING ACROSS THE UNITED STATES IN MOST MAJOR MARKETS. OUR PREMIER LOCATIONS ACROSS THE UNITED STATES HAVE ALLOWED CLIENTS TO SHOWCASE THEIR BRANDS IN THE MOST VITAL, HIGH PROFILE AND BUSY AREAS IN EVERY MAJOR MARKET.

POSTER SNIPING HAS BECOME SYNONYMOUS WITH "HIGH IMPACT" AND "EXPOSURE" WHEN-EVER ADVERTISING AND STREET MARKETING IS THE SUBJECT AT HAND.

WE ALSO OFFER
EVENT PLANNING
NEW PRODUCT LAUNCH
COLLEGIATE MARKETING

NATIONWIDE COVERAGE IS AVAILABLE

PUBLIC RELATIONS:
STREET PRODUCT OFFERS IMAGE AND LIFESTYLE DEVELOPMENT. STREET PRODUCT WILL WRITE AND CIRCULATE PRESS RELEASES, PROMOTE LOCAL OR REGIONAL CD RELEASE PARTIES, AND MUCH MORE.
SERVICES FOR RECORDING ARTIST, MODELS AND ACTORS.

ARTIST DEVELOPMENT:
WE HAVE PACKAGES THAT INCLUDE STUDIO TIME, CHOREOGRAPHY, STAGE PRESENTS, AND VOCAL TRAINING.

ARE YOU AN OUTGOING AND OVER 18? BECOME A STREET TEAM MEMBER

EMAIL: admin@impactstreetteam.com

Design By: Everyway Media 404-246-8086

164

PUBLISH YOUR BOOK

Share Your Story With The World!

Your story is to important to continue collecting dust in the basement, attic or garage. Your story is to important to wait for another publishing house's approval. Your story is to important to wait for the approval of an agent. Your story is to important for you to let fear stop you from achieving your goals and realizing your success.

Do as you were meant to do; take control of your own destiny and fulfill your dreams of becoming a published author. Your book may save a life, inspire another and bring you unparalleled happiness, but only if you take action today!

I am JaWar, author of the fastest selling music business book in Atlanta, the Atlanta Music Industry Connection, Resources for Artists, Producers and Managers. I was making less than $10/hour, working no more than 24 hours a week when the first edition of the Atlanta Music Industry Connection Book was published. As a child I had a strong speech impediment, I stuttered, which made it very challenging for me to speak in public. Today, I conduct workshops and seminars on the business of music and book publishing. More importantly I have created a system and step-by-step process that will enable most anyone with passion, drive and undeniable hustle to print and publish their own book. I consult businesses and individuals just like you on how to publish their fiction, non-fiction and technical books. Set-up your consultation today by contacting me either at 800-963-0949 or emailing me at jawar@mt101.com

Eternal Success,
JaWar

PROSPERITY INTERNATIONAL STUDIOS

EXCLUSIVE STUDIO

Journeyman Makeup Artist TV, Film, Video, Print Runway & Theatre
Skin Care Specialist, Message Therapist & Locktican
Licensed in Chicago & Atlanta w/ Over Thirteen Years Experience
Specializing in The Entertainment Industry

On Location Also Available

Makeup	Deep Tissue
Special Effects	Reflexology
Body Airbrush	Desert Stone Body Wrap
Runway	Detoxifying
Print	Shae Butter
High Fashion	Body Polish
Beauty Facials	Sugar Polish
Acne	Salt Scrub Waxing
Rejuvenation	Eyebrows
Balancing	Bikini
Men Facials	Legs
Aromatherapy	Back
Customized Massage	Personal Image Consulting
Swedish	And More

Contact for an Appointment
pistudioinc@hotmail.com
404-325-3065 or 678-933-8939

Thank you for reading and investing in the second edition of the Atlanta Music Industry Connection Book. I welcome your comments on how I might improve further editions, how the book has helped increase your knowledge base and increased your contacts. Please send your comments to jawar@mt101.com.

Eternal Success & Hotep
JaWar

ABOUT THE AUTHOR

JAWAR

Chief Visionary Officer of Music Therapy 101, a Music Business Conference since 1998, has given informative seminars in Atlanta, Los Angeles and Washington D.C. He created the workshop to identify and share vital information in a step-by-step process necessary for success and ultimate longevity in the music biz with aspiring artists and those willing to be involved in the music industry.

In 2002, JaWar created the MIC (Music Industry Connection) one of the few free all Music Business Publications that serves all genres of music. In just over a year the MIC tripled is circulation, doubled its' page count and increased its' subscription base. When your event demands practical, relevant, and useful information from an enthusiastic speaker who has legitimately "been there" by releasing the Dark Ages II & Paranormal Activity CDs on his independent record company Kemetic Records consider **JaWar; he may be contacted at 800-963-0949,** jawar@mt101.com or P.O. Box 52682, Atlanta, GA 30355, USA.

JaWar provides music business consulting services with an emphasis on marketing & promotions, strategic planning and profit increasing to select businesses and individuals seeking to advance their companies goals and objectives. Whether through one-on-one consultation or in a business group setting, JaWar may help your business become more efficient and effective.

MAIL ORDER FORM

Please mail me the following music business items to help me achieve my goals & realize my potential. I have completed the attached order form and will include a check or money order for my total and mail it payable to:

MUSIC INDUSTRY CONNECTION, LLC
P.O. BOX 52682, Atlanta, GA 30355, USA

Name:

Company Name:

Mailing address:

City: State: Zip:

Phone: Fax:

Email:

Comments:

www.mt101.com   800·963-0949

Item Description	PRICE Per Item	# Of Items	Total
Atlanta Music Industry Connection E-Book	$19.95		
Atlanta's Music Industry Connection Book: Resources for-Artists, Producers, Managers	$19.95		
Atlanta's Music Industry Connection Book: Resources for ARTIST	$19.95		
Atlanta's Music Industry Connection Book: Resources for PRODUCERS	$19.95		
Music Industry Connection The Truth About Record Pools & Music Conferences E-Book	$19.95		
Music Industry Connection The Truth About Record Pools & Music Conferences Book	$19.95		
How to Press 1,000 Retail Ready CDs Without Using Your Own Money Kit	$149.95		
SUBTOTAL	////////		
Shipping & Handling Add $4.00			
GA residents add 7% sales tax.			
TOTAL			

MAIL ORDER FORM

Please mail me the following music business items to help me achieve my goals & realize my potential. I have completed the attached order form and will include a check or money order for my total and mail it payable to:

MUSIC INDUSTRY CONNECTION, LLC
P.O. BOX 52682, Atlanta, GA 30355, USA

Name:

Company Name:

Mailing address:

City: State: Zip:

Phone: Fax:

Email:

Comments:

www.mt101.com   800 ·963-0949

Item Description	PRICE Per Item	# Of Items	Total
Atlanta Music Industry Connection E-Book	$19.95		
Atlanta's Music Industry Connection Book: Resources for-Artists, Producers, Managers	$19.95		
Atlanta's Music Industry Connection Book: Resources for ARTIST	$19.95		
Atlanta's Music Industry Connection Book: Resources for PRODUCERS	$19.95		
Music Industry Connection The Truth About Record Pools & Music Conferences E-Book	$19.95		
Music Industry Connection The Truth About Record Pools & Music Conferences Book	$19.95		
How to Press 1,000 Retail Ready CDs Without Using Your Own Money Kit	$149.95		
SUBTOTAL	////////		
Shipping & Handling Add $4.00			
GA residents add 7% sales tax.			
TOTAL			

170